FANTASY IMPROMPTU

By Vaughn Phelps

V. I. P.
PUBLISHING

First publication 2014   By Vaughn Phelps

COPYRIGHT 2014
Published in America by
V. I. P. PUBLISHING
P.O. Box # 911
Twin Falls, Idaho 83303-911

4

FOREWORD

I don't believe in giving too much away and I hate synopses. I think it's like conducting an autopsy while the patient is still alive and struggling to get off the table. An introduction is like seeing the bride without her make-up, her hair still in curlers and her wedding dress hanging in the closet.

ACKNOWLEDGEMENTS

Cover design by Mitzi Michelle Phelps
Edited by Ginny Greene

CONTENTS

FANTASY IMPROMPTU

STORY ADAPTED FROM THE
SCREENPLAY OF THE SAME NAME
By Vaughn Phelps

Your bookcase can leave dangerous clues.

CHAPTER-1
OKAY, WHAT'S GOIN' ON HERE?

Ryan, rugged athletic look, low profile dresser, studies a candid photo of a pretty teen-aged girl in a demure tennis outfit. He inspects another of the same girl a few years older in black cap and gown. In her eyes is a challenge. A studio pose of her as a beautiful young woman in black sheath and pearl earrings. He returns them to a manila folder and locks the file in his drawer then grabs a worn leather jacket and leaves.

John, thirty-five, fastidious dresser, watches him leave, then moves swiftly into the cubicle. He checks file cabinet and desk, both are locked. Carelessly He knocks over an ivory *Ryan York* nameplate and angrily replaces it.

* * * * * *

In the foyer of Island Classics, on Long Island, blow-ups of the other Theodore Gibbons dealerships—Rolls Royce—Ferrari and—Jaguar, line the walls of this modern building where fully restored classic and exotic cars are offered at commensurate prices. A Sport-Coated man knocks at the door titled: N. SHERIDAN, Sales Manager. He enters without waiting for a reply and casually sprawls in a deep cushioned armchair. Behind the executive desk, the high-backed chair facing out onto the Long Island Sound swivels to face front. Nicky—the woman from the photos—frowns. "You were top salesman last year."

"I've been in the top ten for over twelve years."

"This quarter you've only made your draw once."

"Things have been bad all over."

"I have no control over pesticides on our fruit, foreign investment in American industry or the scripting of professional wrestling."

"I didn't mean—"

"But I DO_control those who work for me and when they DON'T any longer."

A wimpy-looking man knocks, enters, lays papers on Nicky's desk and says, "Three calls waiting, an appointment with the TV producer in half an hour and proofs to be checked before the newspaper can run your latest ads." He leaves.

She waves a graceful hand in a sweeping, dismissive gesture to the man now sitting up straight. "Off you go." Totally ignoring his presence while he's scrambling to regain some measure of self worth, she picks up the phone and, one at a time, places different ads in all the major

New York City newspapers. They all stress the integrity of Island Classics, rather then hawking individual cars.

* * * * * *

At a dark, uncrowded bar, Ryan sips his drink as Sport Coat enters, takes an adjacent stool and reaches for the pretzels. Without turning to look, Ryan places an envelope filled with twenties on the bar.

Sport Coat slides it into his pocket and says, "If she ever finds out I gave you stuff on her private life I'll be out on the bricks."

"You'll be there anyway, if you don't get back to selling cars."

"You're startin' to sound like her."

"You could do worse."

"Who the hell wants to work for a broad, anyway?"

"Not only is she smart and foxy, she's the classiest lady you'll ever meet."

"Stop, before I throw up."

Ryan slips off the seat, throws a ten down on the bar and walks out.

* * * * * *

Mr. Klein, 75, in apartment 705 of the Calcutta Arms, holds the phone to his chest, turns to an old woman. "Mama, we just won a free trip to Europe."

"How, Papa?"

"Some radio station wants to send us to Italy, all expenses paid."

"Why, Papa?"

"I don't know." To the phone, "Why is this being given?" To Mrs. Klein, "It's a promotion for the radio Station, the airline and hotel."

"When, Papa?"

"When do...?" He hangs up. "We have to pack, they're sending the tickets over right away. The trip starts Thursday."

Twenty minutes later, Ryan, with airline tickets in hand, enters the Calcutta Arms. He takes the elevator up to seven, passes adjacent 707 and knocks at 705. The Kleins welcome him, show him to a velvet wingback chair and sit opposite him on the brocaded sofa, holding hands. Mr. Klein takes the proffered pair of airline tickets, holds them tightly and smiles.

Ryan enjoys a cup of their excellent coffee. "This is a very attractive apartment. I notice you have the windows open and this high up it smells as clear and fresh as the air in Idaho." They show him around. "And you say all the other apartments are laid out exactly the same?"

"Yes, but, of course, they don't have my missus to decorate."

Blushing, Mrs. Klein says, "We certainly thank you and the radio station for the trip, Mr. Rogers."

"Not Mr. Rogers, just Sam. It's my pleasure. May I use your bathroom before I leave?"

* * * * * *

The first three classic racers pass the checkered flag and pull in for the award ceremony. The fourth car limps into the Island Classics pit.

Nicky climbs out through the 1939 Jaguar's open window, throws her helmet down and tears off the asbestos facemask. With long blonde hair flowing and eyes blazing, she stalks the crew chief. "I told you that suspension was spongy. You cost me the race."

"You were a lap behind the leader."

"But I only missed placing by inches."

The pit phone rings; a young boy in sponsor ad-covered coveralls that match Nicky's red, white and black team colors, answers and turns. "It's for you, Miss Sheridan."

Angrily, she takes the phone. "This had better be good news."

"That depends on how well you accept success. You weren't expected to make the qualifying heat. Nor to finish among the first twenty."

"If your intent is to encourage, get me a crew chief who follows orders."

"You know I never wanted you behind the wheel of those things anyway."

"I'm not happy with being in the pack and you want a winner."

"You know what I want."

"Ted, we've been over this before."

"We'll discuss it later. A reporter from Race Week is coming by today."

"No. I'll give an interview from the winner's circle. I want publicity only for 1st place cars."

"But, surely you see the advantage of—"

"They'd publish my photo draped across the hood in a bikini. That's NOT what I want."

"Don't take that attitude, Nicky."

"You want press. I want GOOD press. I'd pose that way if I thought that would get it, but it won't."

"Okay, we'll find another crew chief."

"And different carburetors. These flood at low manifold vacuum."

* * * * * *

A Checker Cab drives Nicky from one place to the next. She holds a folded Autos-for-sale newspaper want ad page. The cab stops and waits while a young Queens couple show her a rusty VW Beetle.

Without taking the time to explain her rejection, she climbs back in the cab and continues her shopping tour.

From a Puerto Rican neighborhood estate sale she buys a flame-painted French taxi with no engine.

A lamppost For Sale sign leads her to Harlem where she buys a rusted 1936 Daimler-Benz twin cowl sedan with rat-eaten upholstery and no hood or trunk lid. From a circled newspaper obituary article she buys a 1937 Horsche town car from the widow. At a distance, an auto transport van follows and picks up her purchases.

* * * * * *

John stands before a large desk. A cigar-smoking Pollack, 40, in shirtsleeves and red suspenders, hands him a folder, "Janis Pharmaceuticals."

"I thought you were going to give that to Ryan."

"Well, he's not here so I can't, now, can I?"

"He's never around when there's real work to be done. He snuck out early again."

"I've told you before, I'm not interested in your petty office rivalry."

"It's not—"

"Oh just take this file and get the hell out of here."

* * * * * *

Pushing a low-bed shopping cart in this Help Yourself building material outlet, Ryan selects diverse building materials and tools. The small items fit easily inside the huge trunk of his paint-starved Plymouth. But intent on securing the four-by-eight sheetrock panel on the roof, he wraps the rope around the doorposts.

When he's finished, he looks around and seeing his faux pas, sheepishly climbs in through the window.

* * * * * *

At the Self-Directional Gym, one by one, her classmates fail to grasp the Instructor's attempt to teach them a new throw. Nicky, last in line, finishes the karate demonstration by throwing a large man twenty feet. With clasped hands, she bows to her fallen foe, turns and heads for the showers.

* * * * * *

Mama Leone's waiters tactfully stack the dining room chairs above tables as Nicky intently studies her yellow legal pad notes.

A nearby waiter coughs into his napkin and looking beyond the nearly empty bottle of straw-wrapped Chianti, she's suddenly unaware that the other diners have all left. Checking her diamond Rolex, she smiles, over-tips and gathers her papers into an expensive leather briefcase. Still thinking about directing her next commercial, she climbs the stairs to street level.

Near her apartment three young men, accost her for her purse and jewelry. With two well-aimed kicks forcefully delivered, she puts two of them down, and lines up to take out the next one with a hand edge chop to the Adam's apple. Deciding that perhaps discretion really is the better part of valor, he drags his two inept friends away.

CHAPTER-2
SAFE AT HOME

By streetlight, Ryan reads, "Short, Not So Sweet," a best selling book of short stories that he props against the Plymouth's steering wheel. As a song ends on the car radio, a sultry female voice in a low register announces, "That was Lani Hall's, 'The Look of Love'." He watches Nicky pull a mint-green, open top MG-TD into the garage and park it in her spot. He records the time in a pocketsize notebook.

Minutes later, entering her spotless, apartment, she drops her briefcase and, kicking off her alligator heels, she bends to inspect the $800 shoes for battle damage. Yawning, she throws her silver jacket at a chair. It misses and lands on the floor where it is destined to spend the night. A Betty Crocker cookbook, *Treasure Island*, *Ivanhoe*, *Hiawatha*, *Robinson Crusoe* and *Shipwrecks of the Atlantic*, line the top shelf of the French walnut bookcase. As she heads to the shower, the same radio station plays,

"STARDUST."

* * * * * *

"This is PJ Blegen signing off. To all you single gals; hold this thought—There's a guy somewhere out there for you. Especially you, N.S. Else all your mother's prayers were in vain."

Nicky smiles, turns it off and heads for her large ornately carved walnut bed.

Early the next morning, Jimmy, a small dark Filipino in a white jacket, enters apartment 707. Hearing the shower running, he brews fresh ground coffee, hangs the silver jacket in the closet and sets her briefcase beside the Captain's chair. He irons a stylish red jacket, drapes it over the sofa back, places matching high heels beside it, then serves coffee and juice, makes toast and sets a rose in a crystal vase on a white lace doily at the head of the eight-foot dining room table. He posts a hastily scrawled note in pencil on the refrigerator and lets himself out.

* * * * * *

In stages, Ryan carries his tools and building supplies into apartment 705 of the Calcutta Arms.'

* * * * * *

Nicky shows a large group of executives multi-colored graphs and charts showing that restored classics have been a stable adjunct to the normal sales total and shown larger gross and net profits than new, used car sales, leases, parts or service. She spends the rest of the day creating newspaper and TV ads.

* * * * * *

A middle-aged black hooker with Jerry curls, stands on a Broadway corner, rejects three offers.

The best was six dollars. She keeps watching the white door of a three-story brownstone across the street.

* * * * * *

Late that same afternoon, Ryan enters a theatrical props rental firm and finds everything he's looking for. The young attractive cashier shows interest in his selections, but a much greater interest in him. He doesn't seem to recognize the fact that she's flirting with him.

* * * * * *

In the Le Trianon cocktail lounge, Nicky sits at a nine-inch by nine-inch table and waits. A man, lounge lizard type, slides onto the seat opposite.

"What'cha drinkin,' Gorgeous?"

"As you can see. I'm not drinking, but thank you for your interest.

"You're too beautiful to sit alone. I'll just bring my drink over and—"

"I'm waiting for someone, but I do appreciate your concern."

"It's not cool to wait by yourself."

"I'm not lonesome."

"Yeah, but—"

"Look, I tried being polite. Maybe I'm just not good at it, but even if I did want company it wouldn't be a guy with gold-plated chains, a polyester shirt unbuttoned to his navel and a toop probably made from rat hair, so blow!"

The man starts to respond, but can't find the words.

21

PJ Blegen, in Navy pea coat, huge silver bracelets and earrings, shapely legs in cowboy boots, waves. She brings two drinks from the bar to Nicky's table. "Vodka gimlet for you, same as always."

"What's that you're drinking?"

"Sex On the Beach. It tastes terrible, but who can resist a name like that. I'm trying to wrap my mind around taking two weeks off."

Nicky grins. "So you're finally going to take a vacation?"

"Nah. Well, I could, but I'm afraid they'd replace me with an on-air Dog Psychologist and he'd skunk me in the ratings."

As the early dinner crowd is leaving en masse, the waiter carries their drinks and leads them to their regular booth in the dining room. He takes PJ's coat. Underneath, she's wearing bright red shorts and a flowing Cossack blouse. Nicky is focusing on the clown she had just destroyed. He's trying his line on a middle-aged housewife and it looks as if it's working.

Shaking her head, downing her drink and ordering refills, she says, "Tell me honestly about my personality failings."

"Don't know of any, Hon." PAUSE. "Ex...cept, of course, you intimidate every man who enters your world."

* * * * * *

Near exhaustion, Nicky enters her apartment, turns on the stereo, fills a brandy snifter with Cabernet Sauvignon and reads the refrigerator note.

"MiSSIE NICOLE I go visit mother I tol' you last month. I back three week. You forget my check again. I get when come back. JIMMY"

She takes her wine and legal pad to the sofa. Her large Electro Voice Patrician stereo system plays Wagner. It's a good match because just like her personality, the music goes from the ethereal to the earthy.

When Lohengrin ends, the silence wakes her and, on the way, carries her empty glass to the sink and stumbles to bed.

CHAPTER-3
SOMETIMES JUST THINKING IT MAKES IT REAL

As her three-weight Vienna Regulator strikes midnight, something awakens her and she senses changes in the room's air pressure. Sitting up, she sees moonlight reflecting off a broadsword. Beside her bed, in seventeenth century costume, Ryan stands with legs spread and fists on hips.

"Morgan, the pirate, has cast you adrift for failing to lead him to Black Beard's treasure. Your little raft has been dashed against the rocks of this deserted island. Naked, bleeding and in a coma, you wash ashore. You wake in a hammock under a thatched roof. Lack of food, water and sleep has sapped your strength. I wipe your feverish brow and revive you with a kiss. Feeding you shark soup, breadfruit and rum-soaked coconut and, I..."

Sliding out of the opposite side of the bed, Nicky assumes a defensive pose. "I don't know who you are or what the hell you think you're doing, but get out and go do it somewhere else, or I'll call the police! Wait, I'm sure I locked the door, how did you get in?"

"Make up your mind, Mistress, which do you want first?"

"First, I want you out. On your way out, tell me how you got in."

"You summoned me. Are you sure you want me to go? They didn't mention the inconsistency of the human female, but then…"

"Mentioned? Who didn't mention? And what do you mean inconsistency?"

"That's more questions. If you continue in this fashion we shall never finish."

"You're finished already."

"That's what I mean by inconsistent behavior. I'm here at you're request and—"

"My what?

"You don't recognize me?"

"I've never laid eyes on you."

"Not eyes, perhaps, but then you've never before called me. This is, after all, your fantasy."

"My what?"

"Must I repeat everything? You are too young to be hearing-impaired, but I suppose it could be a genetic fault."

"Now look, I'm open minded, but you won't sell this as some dream."

"A fantasy isn't a dream, although I suppose they do bear certain similarities. But this is not something you wake up from as if it never happened. You have somehow summoned me, and as long as it is your wish, I will remain."

"You mean like some kind of genie?"

"I am not familiar with this term. It is perhaps some form of colloquialism?"

"Okay, I give you points for originality, but it's still no sale, so toddle on out of here."

"I hear and obey. Your climate is far too cold for my taste anyway."

He enters the bathroom. Nicky starts to call out, but waits for him to discover his own mistake. When he doesn't come out, she pulls on a robe and, ready to fight, she stands before the bathroom door. "Did you really think I'd just forget you were in there and go back to sleep?" There's no answer. "Will you come out of there or must I get tough?"

26

With still no answer, she opens the door carefully and turns on the bathroom light, but a thorough investigation proves the room is empty.

The front door is dead bolted. The windows don't open and there's no fire escape to her apartment. She shakes her head.

No more spicy food and wine after a long night at the books.

Taking a swig of Pepto-Bismol and, throwing her robe towards the vanity, she climbs back in bed and turns out the light.

* * * * * *

At Inn Print Books, the next morning, Nicky shops for and buys a book on dream interpretation.

Later, at the weekly sales meeting, Nicky plays a polished, well-directed video commercial, making her case for Island Classics even stronger. The meeting ends, leaving Ted and Nicky alone. He takes her hands in his. "You made this marvelous video on your own? You wrote the script, hired and directed the actor?"

"It was the only way to get it the way I wanted."

"Honestly, I grow more and more impressed with you, daily."

A man is busy painting General Manager in gold lettering on Nicky's door.

* * * * * *

Dressed all in white, a man pulls back white lace curtains and looks out at Broadway, then takes a white swivel chair, holds a white phone to his ear and dials. "There's still nothing new. Go ahead with the original plan."

* * * * * *

On a Miami park bench, Archie, 45—looks 60, with a beer gut, sweat-stained shirt and wrinkled shorts—holds a hand over his ear to block out traffic noise. "Okay, I already got ads runnin'." He hangs up, removes a faded Dolphin's cap and wipes his face and baldpate with a gray handkerchief. Across the street are high-rise, high-priced beach hotels. He crosses between a run down Cuban restaurant and Chinese take out and tacks up the reward posters with Nicky's photo in a Korean nail salon. He leaves some with the cashier of a coffee house. At a community center, he hands them out to senior citizens, and, at the American Legion Post, he tacks some up on the bulletin board. At a closed video rental store, he tapes one to the window.

* * * * * *

At the *Southland Advertiser,* he smiles at a young, attractive Cuban woman. She doesn't smile back. Today, he's dressed in a sweat-stained tropical shirt, plaid seersucker shorts, white sox and sandals. Not a good pick-up outfit.

"You're going to run your ad again, Mr. Fishbine?"

"Another week, yeah."

28

He removes his faded straw hat and sweat from his brow drips into his eyes making him blink.

The woman takes a tear sheet from the rack and circles the photo of Nicky. "Same copy?"

"Yeah. Except bump the reward to two grand."

From a worn and grease-stained wallet, he pulls a wrinkled five-dollar bill and throws it onto the counter. The woman takes the bill to the cash register. She'll run the ad; even though she seems convinced that he couldn't even steal two thousand dollars.

Tacking several to the bulletin bard of a laundromat, he throws the rest of the posters onto the seat of a rusty Gremlin and grinds the starter until the engine catches with a sigh and a puff of smoke.

30

CHAPTER-4
WINNING ADVERTISING

A young tourist couple dawdles over coffee and bagels at the Miami Stage Door Deli. Scanning the *Southland Advertiser, they see* the studio photo of Nicky, captioned "$2,000.00 REWARD for information concerning this woman."

* * * * * *

Across the church entrance, a banner proclaims—
NICKY SHERIDAN—ST. THERESE
ORPHANAGE ALUMNI OF THE YEAR.

She and PJ sit at the Guest of Honor table. On each table are crackers, cheese and wine; Nicky refuses the wine.

PJ grins, "You <u>can't</u> turn this down. It's the finest they've ever served at one of these swell affairs." She reads the label. "Let's see, vintage Tuesday. Much better than what they served me. I think mine was from a 4 PM batch."

"Don't say that. You know you were as honored as am I."

"Yeah. I'm just a little bitter. Here we are the two sexiest, most intelligent and desirable females in the place, and we're both suffering the frustration of Non Cockus Havis."

"What does...? Oh." She puts both hands to her face trying to stifle the laugh.

"Sure, we need a male bod around the House.

Even Sister Elizabeth has Father Donovan to warm her feet." She pours wine for Nicky.

"No, listen. Lately, I've been having a negative reaction to alcohol."

"We'll take a cab, pick up our cars tomorrow. When, unfortunately, we'll be sober."

"But…my problem doesn't start on the road, but after I get home."

PJ pushes the glass into her hand. "So you'll spend the night at my place."

Nicky drinks, takes a 35 mm camera from her purse, and before they start feeling the results of a liquid dinner, she has someone take two shots of the Sisters, one of her and PJ together. PJ takes one of Nicky at the podium.

CHAPTER-5
THAT'S NOT PLAYIN' THE GAME

Much later, in PJ's guest room, decorated in peach colors, Nicky snuggles comfortably in a single brass bed, smiles and drops into a happy sleep.

* * * * * *

Slumped behind the wheel, vibrations of an advancing street sweeper wake Ryan and his head hits the side window with a

THUNK.

He checks his watch, shakes his head, looks across the street at Nicky's empty spot in the garage, stretches, rubs his neck, turns the ignition key and drives off.

* * * * * *

Carrying yogurt and a thermos, PJ, in a green Day-Glo jogging outfit, her hair tied with a red shoestring, enters radio station WAPL. A bouquet of flowers await her at her desk. She enjoys the flowers, but ignores the card.

An hour later, a nice-looking young man, Eddie, pokes his head in and puts everything he can muster into the smile he gives PJ. She's spooning the last of her yogurt. He sees the flowers watered in a wine carafe and the card still unopened.

"Thought I'd try again."

She looks up, frowns at him and goes for the thermos. "What is it this time, Eddie? You want me to meet your family?"

"That too, but, I'll ease you into it, starting with supper at Emilio's."

She shakes her head, as if dealing with a retarded child. "They close at ten and you know I don't sign off until midnight."

"Emilio is a friend. He promised he'd stay open just for us and prepare anything we want."

"Look, Eddie you're a very nice boy. I don't know any woman who wouldn't be flattered by your attention."

"It hasn't worked with you."

"I've told you I'm—"

"Too old for me, I know. Eleven months doesn't scare me."

CHAPTER-6
IF AT FIRST YOU DON'T SUCCEED…

Showered and dressed in a black strapless gown, Nicky empties her daily purse and transfers necessities into a small black clutch bag and, with no room in the 3" by 9" purse, she leaves the camera on her bureau.

From the Plymouth, Ryan watches, sees the cab arrive and Nicky and Ted leaving together.

Ryan checks her still camera's film counter; it's set at 11. He sets it onto her tripod and takes photos of the bedroom, noting his shots on a 3x5 card. Starting at the first shot, 12 is the bed and mirror. The next shows the mirror reflecting against the wall. Others are taken from various positions around the room. He finishes the roll, but before it rewinds to the beginning, manually rewinds to number 11, then puts the camera back in place beside a mini cassette recorder.

* * * * * *

Chez Antoine's treats Nicky and Ted like royalty. Ted refills her champagne glass several times. "You need to relax after a day like today, darling."

"I just want to go home, soak in a tub for an hour, then sleep."

"I'd be glad to…"

"Alone."

"Okay, I just thought a brandy and…?"

"And…?"

"You need a man around the house."

"Thanks, I have Jimmy."

"I could scrub your back."

"I have a long handled brush and I can scrub my own back."

* * * * * *

Fumbling with her key, Ted takes it from her and fits it into the lock of 707. She reaches inside and turns on the light. "Whew, way too much bubbly."

"It was a celebration. You're entitled." He kisses her and obviously wants to come in.

She stops him. "No. We almost made that mistake once before and you're still married."

"But you know Agnes and I are separated."

"We can discuss it again after your divorce is final."

He sees the mini-cam. "What are you going to do with that? We're already up on twelve stations ten times an evening. All in prime time with your tape just as it is."

"That's fine, but the same pitch won't work forever. I want to start on some new ideas. As soon as my head stops spinning."

"You are absolutely incredible."

He kisses her again and reluctantly takes his leave. Undressing as she goes, and dropping clothes like a snake shedding its skin, she heads for bed.

Sometime later, she stirs, tries to roll over, but her foot catches on something. She sits up and turns on the small reading light.

Dressed as Prince Valiant, Ryan is sitting at the side of her bed smiling at her.

"No! Not again. What did I do to deserve this?"

"The Norman invaders have confiscated your father's lands for back taxes. Henry, Prince of Saxony, has demanded your hand in marriage."

"Oh, look, I've notified the police of your perversion, they said—"

"You think you have no one to turn to. But I have just returned from the Crusades. We have until dawn to make it to the long boat. In the shadows, my men await to take us across the channel. In Prussia, friends will help us."

"What is it with you? Do you WANT to be put into a rubber room?"

"If you tell that story, Mistress, 'tis not I will be branded as possessed."

She throws off the covers and again takes a defensive pose.

"Don't blame me, Mistress, if you're unhappy. I'm doing my best to fulfill your fantasy."

"I won't argue, but unless you can prove your ectoplasmic structure, you'll never sell your fantasy story here."

"How do you expect me to…wait a minute, I can't be photographed. Do you have a camera?"

"Yes, there on the bureau."

She watches him set the camera on the tripod. He sets the automatic release, then jumps in front of the lens and duplicates his earlier shots. The camera is always facing away from her, so she can't see that he's left the lens cap on. With his last shot, the camera rewinds automatically.

He removes the film cassette and kissing her palm, drops it into her outstretched hand then disappears again into the bathroom.

The one-hour photo kiosk opens at 7 AM. At one minute after seven, Nicky, holding tightly to a photo receipt, orders coffee at the "Good Old Bean" in the same mall. She opens a travel magazine and keeps reading the same ad for fifty-nine minutes.

CHAPTER-7
SOME TRUTHS ARE HARD TO ACCEPT

At one minute after eight, Nicky makes it as far as the curb before tearing open the photo envelope. She sees herself and PJ, the Sisters, herself at the podium and then her apartment. Prince Valiant is in none of the shots.

At the Inn Print Books, Nicky buys a book titled *The Latent Alcoholic*.

* * * * * *

Just as Ryan is putting on his jacket, Pollack leans into his cubicle. "You leavin' early again?"

"Have to, Chief. Duty calls."

"Duty, my ass. Probably some poor gullible secretary you've convinced that you're a movie producer."

"I only use that line on weekends."

* * * * * *

Alone in her office, Nicky can't decide if she should stay and try to treat the day as normal, go home and curl into a ball or join the Marines.

David, 14, well dressed in hand-tailored suit, silk tie and custom-made oxford shirt, enters the showroom floor and looks over a 1925 Duesenberg Phaeton. He passes that, and shows interest in a 1937 Alfa-Romeo coupe. A salesman watches the boy inspecting a 1926 Isotta-Fraschini limousine.

He grins, saunters over to the boy and talks to him quietly. No, that's not accurate. He listens to the boy and finally leads him to Nicky's office.

"Miss Sheridan, may I present to you, Mister David Boyle. He requests personal attention from you."

Nicky smiles and after engaging introductions, shows him several cars. "I see you in something dashing. Red, perhaps?" She chooses a gull wing Mercedes. He climbs in, but with deep bucket seats, he's unable to slide closer to her. He's smart enough not to say that out loud.

"We have a very nice 1928 Hispano-Suiza limo that was built for a Maharaja who died before paying or taking possession of the car. It then sold to Governor F.D. Roosevelt."

He seems happy enough just to be by her side.

"We have a great car that's almost ready for the showroom. It's a 1932 Marmon two hundred horsepower V-16 once owned by Gary Cooper."

The boy listens intently, as though he has any idea who Gary Cooper is. "No, I'm leaning toward the dark blue convertible in the corner."

With seemingly a deeper appreciation of his maturity and intelligence, she takes a deep breath as she looks down at him. "You have excellent taste. That's a 1939 Delahaye ragtop with a 4-1/2 liter, triple camshaft V-12. You're seeing the original hand-rubbed 16 coats of paint on the coachwork."

He listens and absorbs all the features as she explains everything the car has to offer, but his eyes never leave her. Finally, he says, "Pending a proper test drive, I am prepared to buy at an equitable price."

"Great, I'll have Mr.—"

He shakes his head. "By the deal maker, not some flunky. I will trust you to put the car through its paces."

An awkward silence follows, but Nicky, not about to set the cat among the pigeons, says, "That car is a bargain, only because it's not as well known here as in Europe. The price is $1,050,000."

Without blinking, the boy pulls out a checkbook and as he's writing, says, "In real estate terminology this is called Ernest Money. If I make you an offer that you refuse, you will return the check to me. If without good reason, I balk after your acceptance of my offer, I then default this amount."

He tears out the check and holds it out to her. Still unconvinced, but too intrigued not to see where this is going, she's too stunned to immediately respond. As she reaches for the check, he holds the corner long enough to force her to look him in the eye.

"Naturally, you'll want to check with my bank. Ask for Mr. Borica."

After verifying that, yes, the boy is fully capable of making purchasing decisions in that amount on his own, she motions for a mechanic to have the tires and fluids checked, the car moved out and warmed up. His $25,000.00 "Ernest Money" will be a good day's income if the sale doesn't go through.

There are no flags, tethered balloons or funky thirty-foot inflated waving vinyl giants.

The Island Classics presented to the public is more that of a large bank. The impression is that this is a place to make profitable investments. The half-acre frontage is manicured lawn, not a bunch of used cars with their hoods up like a line of hungry crocodiles.

Watching and waiting patiently, David stands under the wide overhang of the front showroom window.

With a number of questions Nicky returns. He stops her with a simple hand gesture. "We can talk during the test drive."

She's wearing a wispy nylon blend summer dress and the steady breeze off the Sound plasters it against her, clearly outlining her voluptuous body.

Out on the ramp, several service advisors—all dressed in spotless, starched and creased uniforms—dust the car and try not to be obvious as they try to get a look at the kid buying a car none of them could afford after a lifetime of savings.

David jumps into the passenger seat and Nicky climbs behind the wheel of this low-slung, aerodynamically futuristic car that at all-out speed is just a blue blur.

Once on the Interstate she lets the car out and, in second gear the speed quickly climbs past eighty-five. With the top down, the wind captures any conversation, but the engine noise is almost non-existent. The tachometer never passes the three thousand RPM mark yet in less than ten minutes at a steady speed, they have traveled over 15 miles.

She slows the car to take the next off ramp and heads for a DQ.

"I hope you don't mind, but this is the only place around that has carhop service and I love their Kiwi milk shakes."

They sit and sip and, even without words, seem to enjoy each other's company.

As she backs out of the drive-in stall, he makes his play.

"I'll take the car at $950, 000, if you deliver it to me tonight. We can leave now and finalize the deal over dinner. Afterward, my chauffeur will take you home."

"I'm afraid I can't—"

"Really? I thought you were far too astute to turn this down."

He gives her directions to a gated and walled estate with a driveway leading to the mansion at least three hundred yards from the street.

She passes a like new, Bugatti stretch limo, being waxed.

"Drive around back. Erik can put it away while I see to dinner. What food do you prefer?"

A wave of her hand is interpreted as signifying that his selection would have been her choice.

The interior is more like a European castle made into a luxurious hotel. She is led into the drawing room. Dinner is served in about the time one would expect from a fast food place with slow servers. Over Chicken-Kiev and wild rice, she finally asks the questions she's wanted to ask all afternoon. "You came intending to buy a car?"

"I came to buy a car from YOU. I'd seen you on TV driving first that hopped-up Porsche and later the Jag. I learned that you bank at Long Island Commerce and asked Mr. Borica about you."

"The branch manager? Why would he—"

"My father is chairman of Long Island Commerce Bank. Among others."

"And you expected what...?"

"I wanted to meet you. You stimulate within me a strong physical attraction."

"You're what, thirteen, fourteen?"

"In two years I'll be almost seventeen, the peak of a man's performance."

"In four years I'll be...almost thirty."

"A woman's prime."

"I'm flattered, but—"

"You can wait. Surely a few years can't make that much difference. You're busy now with your career anyway."

She starts to respond, but hesitates to form the proper words.

He jumps into the void. "I'm not a spoiled rich kid. I do all right as an arbitrager, but in eight years I come into my own inheritance. With REAL money, you'll want for nothing."

"Where are your parents?"

"My father is in Paris settling another merger."

While he abstains, he refills her glass with a vintage Chateau Rouge. "This is a Claret I picked up in Bordeaux. I'm told it's a fine pressing."

"Your mother?"

"My real mother died when I was two. Since then I've had a succession of stepmothers. All decidedly younger than my father and they seem to be progressively younger all the time.

44

Soon they will pass me, I've no doubt."

"And you've reversed that precedent?"

"Not without good reason. And have you committed yourself to anyone else?"

She clears her throat. "I know you'll be pleased with the car, but I'd get it insured for at least a million before you take it out onto the street."

Looking deeply into her eyes and waiting until she makes eye contact, he says, "That's a total non-sequitur, it avoids my question."

He hands her a check for the car's balance, but holds a corner as she tries to take it from his hand. "Don't say no. Think about it. You can give me your answer when you bring me the car title, Mon Cher."

CHAPTER-8
IF IT WORKED BEFORE, TRY IT AGAIN

The chauffer-driven ride home in the Bugatti gives Nicky time to close her eyes and envision herself marrying a precocious child in a tux with short pants. She pours a generous shot of brandy from the built-in bar. The image won't go away. She takes another shot. The chauffer escorts her to the main entrance and watches her through the barred plate glass door until she makes it to the elevator.

In her own bed earlier than usual, she tries to stay awake, but can't. Her breathing slows as she slips into REM pattern. Her copy of *Hiawatha* slips from her hand. The mini-audio recorder under her bed records her breathing and the steady tick of the Vienna Regulator on the living room wall.

Not much past midnight, Ryan, in fringed and beaded buckskins comes from the bathroom and eases the door closed. He takes the book from her hand, but hesitates when he sees the recorder under her bed, he lifts it, fast forwards to the end where it shuts off automatically. He slips it and an eagle feather back under the bed.

In the starlight from her window overlooking Central Park, a soft murmur comes from a sleepy woman in the beginning throes of foreplay. The bedside light comes on abruptly. Nicky tries to scramble from the bed.

Ryan is laying above the covers, facing her on the pillow, his warm right hand caressing her cheek.

He whispers, "I pull you to shore just before you go under for the third time. The enemy tribe, leaving you for dead, moves south on the opposite bank, searching for survivors to torture or kill.

You start to cry out from the pain of possibly broken ribs. But I clamp a hand over your mouth and slide you under overhanging roots."

She shakes her head. "Oh God! This can't be happening, please…"

"Relax. Stop fighting the inevitable and give in to your inner feelings."

"I don't—"

"Do you deny that all of these fantasies are from your own psyche?"

"They…"

Ryan slips higher on the bed.

"It's not, I mean I never…"

He kisses her neck.

"I don't know."

He kisses her chin and lingers on her lips.

Muffled, "You can't…"

"Can't what?"

She pushes him away. "Let me…no, wait let me think…"

"What is there to think about?"

"Give me a couple of days. I'll summon you."

In a single motion, he climbs off of the bed, slips quietly into the bathroom.

Not at all refreshed, Nicky tosses and turns, trying to fight her way back to sleep, but after four hours of half-sleep she awakens fully, just before sunup. She sits up, shivers and reaches under the bed and retrieves the recorder then sees the feather. With shaking fingers, she pushes the play button and listens, nothing but her soft breathing.

Wide-eyed, she staggers into the bathroom and hopes a cold shower will revive her. At best, it gives her goose bumps all over.

Later that morning, Nicky enters a brownstone. The brass plaque beside the door reads, Millicent Browder-Family Psychiatry: By appointment only.

* * * * * *

At Western Union, Ryan hands the clerk cash, the clerk fills out a form and gives him a receipt. He leaves.

* * * * * *

Mr. Klein, waving a telegram, joins Mrs. Klein at the Trevi Fountain. "Look, Mama. The radio station sent money for another week's stay."

* * * * * *

Walking briskly down a tree-lined street, Ryan, passes several stores. A few pre-teen boys on the corner play catch with a dead tennis ball. He detours into an ice cream parlor, speaks to the clerk, hands him cash and leaves. He's a block away, not looking when the clerk hands triple-decker cones to all the kids. As he passes a dry cleaners, he overtakes a stooped older black woman with two shopping bags. He slows, falls in step with her, carries her bags and walks her two blocks to her door. She mumbles and takes one of the bags; Ryan keeps the other. Inside her second floor apartment, Roxie stands up straight and pulls off her gray wig.

She hands Ryan her surveillance log.

* * * * * *

At Emilio's, Eddie leads PJ down the steps.

At the bottom, she pulls away and says, "Look, this is dinner and that's all."

"Of course."

"And I'm not going to any dumb softball game with you Saturday."

"Certainly not." He takes her coat and holds out a chair for her.

CHAPTER-9
AT 200 MILES AN HOUR, ONE SHOULD CONCENTRATE

Ignoring, as best she can, the noise, dust and frantic activity in the pit, Nicky zips up a new fireproof jump suit. A man in matching attire, "Kelly-Crew Chief" over his left breast, helps her into the window of the Lotus racer. "Now remember, the suspension is much tighter for these time trials."

"I'm glad you've taken over; I feel more confident already."

"I only agreed to try it, see if we can work together. Racing is a team effort. Not the normal employee/employer relationship."

"You've crewed some of the best teams ever."

"Take a couple of warm-up laps. Let's see how you do."

Smiling, she stuffs her mass of blonde hair into a crash helmet that looks like an iron mask, then drives onto the track. She does several laps and then returns to the pit.

"That's okay for the freeway, but you're holding back." He looks into her eyes. "Are you all right? Your eyes are dilated."

"I didn't get much sleep last night. I took a super caffeine drink to wake up. I'll do better at the trials."

* * * * * *

At The Fresh Bean, PJ, carefully balancing two whipped cream topped coffees to the tiny table, takes the photos from Nicky's envelope and glances at them.

"I don't see why you're so uptight. These show nothing. Wall, bureau, empty bed, door to the bathroom, door to—"

"Not empty bed?"

"Yeah, empty bed, door to—"

Nicky grabs the prints, studies the only shot of the bed. Slowly and carefully placing them back onto the table as if handling a piece of museum quality ceramic ware, she grins.

"Now what? I know you. When you get that look it means trouble."

"Nonsense. I just realized that I'm not really a fantasy figure."

"Down, girl. You're very attractive, but let's maintain a sense of reality."

"No, listen." She plays her mini recorder of her breathing, the clock ticking.

PJ nods, "Real top forties stuff; you want what? For me to play this on the air?"

"Would you mellow out a moment? What do you hear?"

"Breathing, a clock of some kind."

The tape continues to play.

"No voices? No man's voice? Right?"

"You play a tape with no voices, show me photos of no one and that upsets you. Girl, you've slipped a cog. Let me give you the name of someone who can help."

"You don't understand. I was on the bed, but I'm not in the picture. The tape starts with my breathing and the clock."

52

"Right."

"But, then I fell asleep. You can hear my breathing and the clock."

"Very significant. Should we call the F.B.I.?"

"But then here listen, you can't hear the clock ticking, but it never stopped. The time was right this morning.

"Marvelous. What's all that mean?"

"I think it means I'm not dreaming, not having D.T.'s and I'm not crazy."

* * * * * *

During her afternoon exercises, PJ's phone buzzes and she retrieves the voice messages. "See Sister Elizabeth. You dropped your wallet at the presentation the other night."

* * * * * *

Naively, PJ tries to retrieve her wallet and get away without having to answer any embarrassing questions. Then, before she can escape, Sister Elizabeth rounds the corner into the office.

"PJ, it was so good to see you both again after ten years. It's a shame we weren't able to spend a little private time. I'm always interested in how my girls are doing. A cup of tea would be—"

"Sister, I really have to go."

"Yes, I understand. Your husband must be waiting, children to pick up, that sort of thing."

"No, actually—"

"I always knew you would be the first to settle down with a nice boy. Is he Catholic?"

"No, he's, I mean..."

"What about that tea?"

With a deep sigh…"I guess."

Sister Elizabeth pours. PJ tries to hurry things along. Nothing seems to go that way. After half an hour of small talk the tea and conversation seems at an end. PJ is turning toward the exit, when…

"Did that nice man ever contact Nicole? He seemed so intense, I thought at the time—"

"What man, Sister?"

"Why, the man asking about her, oh, two months ago, or was it three?"

"What man was asking about Nicky?"

"No, it was seven weeks ago. The same week Father Donovan had his appendix out. Sister Margaret Rose said she was going to send flowers from the Order, but she forgot."

"Sister…"

"You remember how Sister Margaret Rose was years ago?"

"Yes, but…"

"Well, she's even more forgetful since Sister Dorcas passed."

"Sister! The MAN?"

"Oh, you know, the man from…now was it…no, not the police, I'm sure of that. He was too nice-looking for a policeman. An investigator of some kind is all I remember. He had the whitest teeth and the most roguish smile."

"SISTER, who was he? Who sent him?"

"I don't really recall. I have his card somewhere, Brian, I think. But, it's unimportant. He said he'd contact Nicole directly."

PJ suffers through another half hour of reminiscence before Sister Elizabeth can be worked toward her knitting basket and the man's business card.

* * * * * *

PJ starts her radio show with Frank Sinatra's,

"THE LAST DANCE."

"So, girls, don't miss the right connection by turning that guy down just 'cause he's not the picture you've held in your head since your pre-teens. Give him a chance; you may be surprised."

* * * * * *

In his office, Ryan adds an electronic notepad, the Sheridan, N. file, to an old briefcase. He fingers a snub-nosed Colt Diamondback, decides to leave it. He locks it, with the studio photo of Nicky, in the top drawer.

CHAPTER-10
THERE'S A SCIENTIFIC
EXPLANATION FOR EVERYTHING

Distracted and in a hurry, Nicky drops one of her pearl earrings, searches the bathroom's tile floor between the full-length mirror and the toilet. Not finding it in the shadows, she gets a seldom-used flashlight. It has corroded batteries. She finds a matchbook and, on hands and knees, holds a match to the dark corner. Just as she sees the earring, the match flickers as it passes the mirror frame. Inches above the floor there's an even crack along the bottom of the mirror. Inserting a hair clip into the crease, she trips a latch, the mirror springs open and she steps into the Kleinses bathroom.

In her seventh floor hallway, Nicky sees a small woman with a beautiful white borzoi about the size of a small pony. "Oh, Mrs. Lucchi, the manager says the Kleins are in Europe. Do you know if they sublet?"

"Oh no, dear, they would never do that."

"Okay, thanks." Nicky starts into her apartment.

"But that nice young man apartment sitting must have a strange job."

"What man?"

"And a very hard worker he is. Comes in late, when I'm giving Boris his evening walk."

"Can you tell me what he looks like?"

Mrs. Lucchi, in minute detail unmistakably describes Ryan.

* * * * * *

Nicky and PJ ride horses along a roped-off equestrian trail through Central Park.

"Nick, I know pearl earrings are all your mother left you, but, they don't go with everything. Especially not a riding habit."

With a secretive smile even she didn't know she possessed, she starts to respond, then repents that idea.

Two attractive men approach, wanting to ride along. Distracted, Nicky keeps to herself. The men take the hint that they're not being invited to share a ride and...maybe something else. They drift off by themselves.

"Hey, those were hunks; you could have at least smiled." Irritated, PJ sulks for a few seconds. That's as long as she can absent her effervesant personality. She fumbles in her farmer's coverall pocket for the card, pulls it out and holds it out to her best friend. "Here, I don't know what it means, but, this guy was asking Sister Elizabeth about you."

"What?"

"It's why I had you meet me today."

Nicky reads the card:

Ryan York, Atlantic Investigations

She turns her horse and gallops back to the barn.

* * * * * *

An hour later, at Atlantic Investigations, Nicky approaches a very attractive young woman, Lisa Ferriday—nameplate on the high counter. She looks up and offers a fake smile."

"May I help you?"

"Mr. York, please."

She studies an in/out board. "He's not signed out, but he often uses the side door to the garage. Let's check his desk."

On the desk below the counter, Nicky sees a silver-framed photo of Ryan. It's inscribed "To Lisa with love, Ryan."

They work their way over to Ryan's office; see a clean desk and empty coat rack. "He may come in any minute; then again, he might be gone for days."

"May I wait? I'm on lunch break. I'll just sit here and have my yogurt."

"Sure, make yourself comfortable. There's coffee down the hall."

Nicky takes the padded chair and as soon as Lisa is out of sight, she tries the desk drawers and files. Both are locked. She uses a stag-handled letter opener the size of a hunting knife on the top desk drawer. The front splinters and pops open. The "Sheridan, N." file holds only the studio photo of her. She props it against the desk lamp and slips the Diamondback into her purse.

Lisa returns. "I just heard Mr. York left for Florida. I can't say for how long."

"Then I guess I'll have a normal three thousand calorie lunch."

"May I tell him you called?"

"It wouldn't mean anything to him. We've never been formally introduced."

"Or what it's about?"

"I think I'd rather surprise him."

* * * * * *

Archie yells through the speaker hole in the bulletproof glass of the U-Pump station.

"You called about the poster in the laundromat?"

The acne-faced boy sizes him up while ringing up a purchase. "Yeah, two grand for information? Not her folks put you up to it, huh?"

"I don't understand what..."

"I mean, she's my old lady, but I ain't knocked her up or nothin'."

"You say the woman in the poster is your wife?"

"Nah, we ain't married, we just like shackin' up, you know?"

"And how old is this woman?"

"Same as me, nineteen. Here's her pitcher."

"Thank you."

He looks, hands the photo back and starts back to his car.

"Hey, what about the two..."

At a poorly maintained cottage in the outskirts of Miami, Archie knocks and must wait only a few seconds before a woman, obviously excited about something, opens and smiles.

"Mrs....Wallace?"

"Come in, Mr. Fishbine. Can I offer you iced tea?"

"No, thank you. Your message said you recognized the photo I ran."

"Yes, I'm sure it's Miss Miller, my doctor's receptionist. Do I get the reward now?"

"I'll have to check it out first. What's the name and address of your doctor?"

Archie enters the office of Daniel Cox, Doctor of Podiatric Science.

The receptionist looks a little like Nicky might in ten or more years and with an extra hundred pounds.

There aren't many mobile home parks in downtown Miami, but Archie is unlucky enough to find one that must have been in place before the advent of modern conveniences like electricity, indoor toilets and brooms.

He checks with a woman in a single-wide. She looks very much like Nicky. She might even be mistaken for her. If only she wasn't a foot shorter.

A road-flag woman looks quite a bit like Nicky except for skin like dried parchment.

A 1st grade teacher with a broken nose has, otherwise, a similar bone structure.

A parking attendant looks the least like Nicky. Archie doesn't even bother referring to the photo.

Not much of an athlete, Archie at least dresses as if he's a bowler. He enters the dimly lit Bowlarama and, as if he fully expects this to be another false lead, he heads dejectedly for the bar. Along the way he passes a bulletin board that lists all the tournament leaders, raffle-drawing winners, and beside them is a photo of the waitress of the month, Martha Washoski. The face that stares back at him is a perfect duplicate of Nicky. He takes a dark corner and orders a beer from the tired waitress. "You got a waitress named Washoski?"
"What'cha want her for?"

"I owe her some money. I was told she ran drinks here nights."

"Giveit ta me, I'll get it to her."

"I could ask around, maybe find someone more cooperative."

She jingles coins on her tray. "Ya know how life works?"

"How about I wait outside at quittin' time." He opens his coat, exposing a .45 auto. "I could, like, refresh your memory."

"Hey mister, I want no trouble. I got a kid and—"

"Just tell me about Washoski."

"She starts at 4, works till 2 AM."

At shift change, Archie nurses a warm beer for two hours until finally his vigilance is rewarded when Martha, (very short skirt, fishnet stockings, rundown heels, and a hip swing that in a narrow hallway would hit both sides), enters, ready for work. Except for peroxide hair and overdone and poorly applied make-up, she's a ringer for Nicky. They talk for a while then Archie shows her a cash envelope. She runs her hands lovingly over the bills. He puts the envelope back in his wrinkled jacket (his best), firmly grips her elbow and leads her outside.

CHAPTER-11
LIFE IS MORE THAN A CHECKERED FLAG

Nicky takes the checkered flag and pulls into the winner's circle, receives roses and a huge Pocono Speedway trophy. David Boyle, in a box high above, cheers wildly. She spots him, waves back and throws him a kiss.

Showered and changed, she enters the Pocono Speedway Diamond Club and spots PJ, sitting with a handsome young executive type. PJ leaves him and joins Nicky at a small table. Toasting Nicky with champagne, she nods her head toward the man she'd just left and says with a smile that contains a lot of venom, "He's so cute, an investment banker. He makes so much money he doesn't count it, he weighs it. His wife is in Connecticut. He wants a sweet little thing to decorate his Sutton Place condo. That's his opening line, the jerk."

"Seems to me, there was a time you'd have thought that was being direct, honest."

"Why are all the good ones either married, gay, both or…?"

The waiter brings Nicky a bouquet of red and white roses. She reads the card, *"Congratulations, we both knew you could do it. David."*

"…too young."

With her eyes fixed-focus, Nicky drifts off to another dimension, trying to solve a question.

He only hits when I'm vulnerable, half snockered and stressed by some big event. The Classic Show Sunday means another fantasy Saturday night."

PJ shakes her head, "You need rest, girl. The pressure of living alone has finally gotten to you. I have no idea what's going on. You want to tell me from the beginning?"

"After I work it all out for myself."

* * * * * *

Archie and Martha leave the "arriving flights" gate at Kennedy International Airport and hail the Traveler's Rest Hotel Shuttle.

* * * * * *

Admiring her first major, trophy Nicky puts her cell phone on speaker and does a slow burn. "I don't understand why I can't speak to him now."

"I told ya, lady. He's busy, we got more than the usual number o' kooks tonight. The lieutenant will get back to you."

"Look, I assure you that I'm not—"

"Yeah, I'll put ya on hold. If he gets to ya, he gets to ya."

Nicky waits. Eventually, with the delay, she moves from hot to erupt.

* * * * * *

Twenty minutes later, she stands before the NYPD Community Relations desk.

64

"Miss...?"

"Sheridan. I gave all the pertinent data to the sergeant."

"Yes, well, when he heard what this was about he stopped writing."

"You expect me to repeat it all?"

"I think I have the gist of the matter. This Peeping Tom shows up late at night and—"

"It's more than peeping."

"Yeah, now let me see. You're single, live alone, got home late, you'd been drinking before each alleged episode and this guy recites poetry."

"Not poetry, the classics. He's made up fantasies from my own library."

"He's some kind of a ghost who disappears like smoke?"

"No. I can show you what I mean physically when you come."

"And you think he'll try again Saturday night?"

"I'm sure of it. Around midnight."

"Okay, we'll send a man by around eleven."

"But, I want to give you all the new material I've gathered before you come to arrest him."

"Well, it'll keep until then. We have your address. Now excuse me, I have a desk full of serious cases."

* * * * * *

This cheap generic motel is one that you just know is more than comfortable charging an hourly rate. Archie looks from the studio photo of Nicky to the real life Martha Washoski, applying lipstick before the cheap, peeling mirror.

"Nah. Still too much; it's all over your face again."

"Listen, I know what guys like."

"You want the five G's or not, Martha?"

She takes the photo from Archie, frowns and studies it.

* * * * * *

Using the tripod and mini-cam, Nicky records herself in the open hidden door. "These are part of the planned operation of a scheming investigator. This mirror was made into a secret entrance. He used it first on the twentieth." She sets the tripod and camera in her closet, covers it with clothes, and aims it at the bed. Then speaking into the camera, says, "Saturday night, I'll use this remote and record his latest fantasy. When the police arrive I'll hand over this tape and the other hard evidence to them."

* * * * * *

At Archie's run down Miami apartment building, Ryan rings the manager's bell and hopes she can hear it. A tired-looking woman perks up when she sees him. He hands her a hundred-dollar bill.

"He's gone. I didn't miss him till this morning."

"Can I take a look?"

"Sure." She opens a messy apartment. Ryan searches, finds a list of women's names. The last name, Martha Washoski, Bowlarama, Southwind Blvd., is the only one not crossed out.

As he enters Bowlarama, Ryan scans the bulletin board, sees the photo of Martha Washoski in uniform, "Employee of the Month." When he takes a stool at the bar seconds later, the photo is no longer on the board. "Club soda, please."

* * * * * *

In her office, Nicky tries to concentrate on the sales reports, but every time she looks out the window, she sees an image of Ryan hanging from a gallows, his eyes closed and swollen tongue hanging out. He's slowly twisting in the slight breeze off the Sound.

* * * * * *

Back at Kennedy, Ryan distributes Xerox photos of Martha and Archie among cab drivers.

* * * * * *

At an up-scale Boutique, Archie and Martha shop the aisles. Her hair is now Nicky's color and style. She browses among flashy dresses. Time after time, he's forced to lead her to a rack of semi-conservative business suits. He cringes at the prices.

* * * * * *

Being led to her front row stadium seat, PJ, wearing a Midnight Blues cap, holds Eddie's coat. He brings her a beer, hot dog, peanuts and cotton candy.

She doesn't draw attention to herself by applauding, but try as she may to hide it, whenever Eddie comes to bat, her eyes shine and she sits forward.

* * * * * *

Martha walks across the motel room, pours two glasses of Scotch and takes one to Archie.

"Ya still got too much bump and grind. Try it again."

She sighs, tries a non-provocative gait. Drinking her Scotch as she walks confuses her and she loses her attention and her balance.

CHAPTER-12
VENI, VIDI, VICI! WELL, MAYBE NOT

Early Saturday evening, Nicky enters her apartment, throws her keys on the small mahogany hallway table and stops dead in her tracks. The dining room table is set, candles are lit, and tuberoses fill the whole apartment with an exotic aroma. Ryan stands over the stove wearing her black lace see-through apron. The stereo plays Chopin's,

"FANTASY IMPROMPTU."

She stiffens. "Chicken Kiev, my favorite? How did you...? Wait a minute. What are you doing here so early? You never come before midnight."

"I come whenever you beckon."

"But..."

"But, what? You've already eaten?"

"No, but…"

He pours chilled Chablis, takes her in his arms and gently kisses her. She resists, but not forcibly. "You called me early this time because you knew we had important things to discuss."

She checks her watch. There are over five hours to stall him until the police arrive. He kisses her again, against even less resistance.

After dinner, Nicky, nervous and distracted, sees in her wine glass an image of Ryan in jail, a marked pervert. "Look, your little charade is up. I was intrigued, but the better part of valor is discretion. Fold your tent and slip away.

You can live to pull this on some poor little farm girl."

"You can't get anything worthwhile by running from it."

"You won't leave?"

"I thought we'd spend a quiet evening together, talk, have dinner and listen to Chopin."

* * * * * *

Half an hour later, Nicky parks her MG under the twenty-foot tall Erotic Nights Motel XXX-rated neon sign.

Ryan is able to partially see through the poorly chosen material with which she's blindfolded him. At full attention he says, "Are you sure this is what you want?"

"I told you. My fantasy can't really be fulfilled at the apartment. Wait for me here and promise you won't take off the blindfold. I'll only be a minute." She registers as Mr. and Mrs. DeSade and rents red-feathered handcuffs. Guiding him to their room blindfolded and now handcuffed, she drags him to the rubber-sheeted round waterbed. She sets the mini-cam tripod to photograph him then uncovers his eyes.

He seems surprised, but not greatly shocked. "I never figured you this kinky."

"I warned you that it was over. Why didn't you just leave when I gave you the chance?"

"If I was going to leave I'd never have come in the first place."

"Why did you?"

"I was about to tell you that tonight, over cognac."

70

"It may be too late for that now. I've already notified the police."

"You threatened me with that before."

"This time I really did it."

"Did they believe you?"

"Not really; that's why I had my collected evidence ready."

"What evidence?"

"Your plants. The photos had me fooled until I realized that I was on the bed, should have been in one shot, but I wasn't."

"So, either we were both figments or neither was?"

"Right. The tape and feather were good, they almost threw me."

"So what tipped you?"

"The clock. The ticking stopped when you fast-forwarded."

"You'd make a good detective."

"Thanks, I also have your secret door on video."

"I was going to fix that Monday. I never expected it to last this long. I figured you'd go two times max."

She starts the mini-cam. "You didn't research me thoroughly enough. Why was my file empty?" She waves his business card at him.

"That was you? I thought it was John, he's after my job."

"He'll get it while you're enjoying life at Ossining's river retreat."

"You don't know any more about this now than you did at the start."

"I will before I'm through."

He studies the overhead mirror and red-flocked walls. "Quite a place. Do you come here often?"

"No, but I thought you'd enjoy the symbolism. This place was built on fantasies."

"The police won't believe you. It's all too subtle. Without motive they won't even write up a complaint."

"I figure you'll confess your motive."

"No. I was going to tell you earlier, now my pride's at stake."

"I'll make you tell me."

"You can try. Three years of POW torture couldn't."

"They don't have my methods."

She unbuttons her blouse, keeps her back to the camera, and slides onto the bed beside him. She kisses him, tears his shirt open. He smiles as if he's enjoying it. She pulls her skirt up to her waist, showing black lace bikini panties that match her bra and slides her right leg over him. Comfortably straddling him, she looks down and with a tone of authority, says, "Tell me your plan and I'll let you go."

With his hands cuffed together, he swings his arms up over her head and pulls her down on top of him. "I think there's a little something about the basic concept of torture that you have failed to grasp." The shrill sound of many

POLICE WHISTLES

break the mood.

With yellow Day-Glo N.Y.P.D. VICE lettering on nylon jackets, burly cops break in.

"Don't move, kids. This is a bust."

She smiles, "It's about time. I was beginning to think you weren't coming."

"Sure. Hands behind your back, lady."

"No, I'm the one who called you."

"O' course."

"I left a note in the apartment. Didn't Lt. Moore follow me from there?"

"There's no Lt. Moore in vice."

"No, I think he's in community relations."

He slips cuffs on her and lifts her off Ryan. "This guy don't need cuffs she beat us to it, Sarge."

"Huh, she don't look the type."

"Proves you never can tell."

CHAPTER-13
IF I DID EVERYTHING RIGHT, THEN WHY AM I HERE?

Ted bails Nicky out. She refits her ever-present pearl earrings through pierced ears. Outside, he leads her to his car and says in a comforting tone, "I don't understand any of this and the media has been given no specifics, but until it's cleared it would be best if you took a leave of absence."

She pulls back. "Don't you want to know what happened?"

"This is not the time or place. I'll...call you."

"I think until I feel you've accepted my word that I did nothing illegal or immoral, it would be best if you took a flying leap at the moon. I'll clear out my office and pick up my severance package."

With his nose in the air and a feeling of righteousness, he leaves. Nicky walks back into Central Booking and phones PJ.

* * * * * *

A long half hour later, PJ, wearing Eddie's leather Midnight Blues baseball jacket, brings dark glasses, a floppy hat and raincoat to get Nicky away without being recognized.

"Thanks for coming. You're a lifesaver."

"Your bail was only a thousand, here's the other thousand, but I didn't have that much cash handy. I had to borrow it from a friend. But I don't understand what...?"

Nicky sees Eddie sitting patiently behind the wheel of a tricked out CJ Jeep. She returns to the booking clerk.

"I'd like to post bail for Mr. York, arrested in the Erotic Nights Motel sting."

He checks the booking sheet. "Mr. York made bail a few minutes ago."

"How did he raise the cash?"

"He called several friends upstairs. They chipped in."

"You mean cops?"

"Maybe you haven't noticed, lady. This a Cop Store."

"Oh, do you have his home address?"

"I can't give out that information."

Nicky climbs into the back seat of the Jeep. She nods at Eddie and asks PJ, "Who's this?"

PJ climbs in, rides shotgun. She wipes her lipstick from Eddie's grinning face. "A friend. Ignore him and he'll go away. Are you going to tell me what you're into?"

"I've been trying to tell you all along, but the game just went into overtime."

Eddie walks them to PJ's door, kisses her, starts off, then comes back to get his jacket and another kiss. Nicky disappears into the apartment, giving them some privacy. He's half way down the stairs when PJ calls him back and takes her wallet and lipstick from his jacket pocket. He gets another kiss.

* * * * * *

76

Ryan sits stoically the next morning as Pollack reads the arrest report and John's private file on Ryan. "John, you say Ryan's been keeping a secret file. Why?"

"I don't know, but the withheld information is locked in his files."

"If you can prove that, do it. If you fail, I'll accept your resignation as of today."

"But—"

"You've been after his spot a long time. Now it's put up or shut up time."

John breaks the lock on Ryan's file cabinet, finds nothing and only Nicky's empty file in his desk. With chagrin on his face, he takes it back to Pollack's office.

* * * * * *

Ryan arrives and is called into Pollack's office.

Frowning at Ryan, Pollack says, "I want to know why you've withheld information from a client."

"I can't tell you that. Not right now."

"You realize I have no choice, then, but to terminate you."

"It's what I'd do in your place."

At the same time, Nicky enters the foyer and smiles at Lisa. "Mr. York?"

"He's in with Mr. Pollack. Would you care to wait?"

"Yes, thank you."

She leads the way to Ryan's office, shows Nicky to a seat. "Can I get you coffee?"

"No, but thank you anyway."

Without rising from her chair, Nicky's eyes search the small space. Other than Ryan's desk nameplate, there is practically nothing of a personal nature. Ryan enters, sees Nicky in the chair watching him. "I'll make a call, then we'll have coffee and talk."

"Talk! That's all? I want some explanations."

"A person gets that by talking and...listening. And I think over coffee works best."

"Sure. Where I won't embarrass you in front of your friends and co-workers?"

"I don't give a damn about that. Besides, I've just been fired. Now, do you want answers or would you rather make a scene?"

She opens her mouth, but has no retort handy.

"There's a good place for both talking and coffee at the Ground Round. It's not far."

He puts the few personal belongings and a folder marked "Uncle Ben" into his worn briefcase as he dials. Into the phone, he asks, "Any word?" PAUSE. "Okay, let me know as soon as you hear." He heads out, reaches back for Nicky. "Come on, let's get to that coffee."

* * * * * *

At a large conservative office, a receptionist switches a call to Franklin Toole.

"Franklin Toole, Claims. How may I be of help, Mr. Pollack?" PAUSE. "Yes, I have that case." PAUSE. "But, Mr. York of your office assured us that..." PAUSE. "Yes, I see. Well, I'll wait for your package." PAUSE. "No, don't fax it; send it special messenger."

78

CHAPTER-14
IS IT REALLY WORTH THE COST?

In the foyer, John has left the inner door open and heard Pollack's phone conversation. In his own small wall-less cubical, he holds Nicky's empty file and dials a memorized number. When it's answered, he says in a subdued tone. "That matter in which you expressed interest has just blossomed into flower." PAUSE. "No, I'm afraid it's too late for that." PAUSE. "Exactly, just a few moments ago. I had no choice. I didn't realize he'd been so thorough." PAUSE. "No, I'm afraid I cannot do that."

* * * * * *

Ryan shows Nicky, with her mini-cam, into his clean, not overly neat apartment. "I came home to get the cash, then went back to bail you out, but you were already gone." He adds a beeper to his belt. "Let me just get some papers, then..."

PAUSE

Through the window he sees a car parking. "Those men are looking for me. But they couldn't already know we're together."

"We're not together."

"Don't quibble over semantics. I'll lead them away."

"I don't believe any of this. You want to just give me the straight skinny for once?"

"You stay here. I'll double back."

He grabs his briefcase and dashes out.

At the window, Nicky sees neither Ryan, nor anyone suspicious. She searches his apartment, finds a legal pad with scale drawings for the closet mirror's replacement, photos, and dimensions for cutting the sheetrock, measurements of her apartment, receipt for air and hotel expenses for the Kleinses.

Videotaping it all, she adds her own acid comments, "We are in the apartment of Ryan York and as you will see, the details of his devious plan are abundantly clear." She dials her own number to recover voicemail.

"Please leave your name, number, time and date. I'll return your call as soon as possible."

BEEP.

(PJ's voice.) "Nick, I'll call you on Monday. I'll be away for the weekend. Bye, Hon."

It's the only message, so she hangs up, takes his keys and her camera and walks out looking for a cab. There's nothing yellow in sight.

At a Wi-Fi café on the corner, Nicky takes a double cherry cone with chocolate sprinkles to a table and dials her own password into the computer. On line, she scrolls through unknown/unwanted messages that her spam filter has missed. One seems intriguing; she opens it.

To: Ms. Sheridan
From: Frank   Toole,
Commonwealth   Insurance
Building,

Commonwealth Insurance Building, Fifth and Wall, Suite 2700

Message:
If you would stop in at your earliest convenience, I would appreciate it. It pertains to a matter of some urgency."

She saves it, hangs up, goes back to get Ryan's Plymouth and drives it up Wall Street to Fifth.

* * * * * *

Mr. Toole meets Nicky at the receptionist's desk and leads her into his spacious office. "So good of you to come, Ms. Sheridan. We've been searching more than two years for you."

"How did you find me?"

"Our own investigators tried and failed. We turned to a private concern."

"Atlantic Investigations?"

"Yes. They have a man there named York who is a whiz at such things. Can you prove your date of birth, family history and answer a battery of questions?"

"Why should I? I don't have a policy with you people."

"Possibly a relative of yours did."

"I have no relatives. I grew up in an orphanage."

"Can you prove that?"

"Of course."

"This afternoon, possibly?"

"Possibly."

"What time may we expect you, Ms. Sheridan?"

"I can make it by three." She starts out, passes a steno's desk; sees the same photo of Ryan inscribed: to Mary with love, Ryan.

* * * * * *

The motel phone rings. Archie, in shorts and mismatched sox, answers. "Slow down. When? Okay, I'll work it out." PAUSE. "I said I'd work it out, now get off my ass. Unless you want to handle it yourself."

PAUSE.

"What I thought. I got two guys on it. I just gotta pull the plug when the time comes. Gimme the address."

Martha comes from the bathroom wrapped in a towel. He scribbles Calcutta Arms on a pad, hangs up and frowns at Martha. "That bitch is still alive."

"What now?"

"I don't know, I gotta' think."

"I still get the money you promised?"

CHAPTER-15
THINGS GET TIGHT

A half-hour later, Ryan, on foot, heads back to his apartment for Nicky. As he passes the Wi Fi café, he sees his Plymouth not where he'd parked it. He climbs in and honks then opens the passenger door. Nicky leaves the Café, bringing her coffee in a "Wireless World" thermal mug, and slides in beside him.

"Boy, I thought I knew automotive elegance."

"I can see the envy in your eyes."

"Where'd you go?"

"I told you there were…"

"Yeah, yeah, guys after you. I didn't buy that."

"Why'd you take the car to only go a block?"

"Oh, I went more than a block. I came back to see if you were the detective some naive people claim you are."

"Well, I found you."

"No, you found the car right where even a blind pig could find it. Some detective."

* * * * * *

Clancy's Bar is not what one thinks of as a coffee bar, but then, one never knows. Ryan shows Nicky to a booth.

She looks around. "Lovely place. I'd say the last time the walls were even dusted was just before British troops sacked the city."

The stocky, shorthaired woman bartender brings two coffees, plops them down on the table. "This her?"

Ryan just frowns at her.

"The one you been changin' your lifestyle for?" Laurie, Toni and Veronica all been complainin' you never call anymore. I figured..."

Nicky smiles at Ryan, "Is this your mother or your father?"

Clancy grins. It's not something she does often. "Oh, this one's got attitude."

Ryan smiles as if he's introducing his two gladiators, "And she knows Karate. Nichole, this is Clancy, Clancy, Nicky."

"I don't guess they call you nickel. Not the way you're dressed." To Ryan, "I think she can handle you."

Nicky starts to answer, but Clancy walks away. Roxie enters, takes a stool at the bar, gives Nicky an appraising look and gets a headshake from Ryan. Ryan sips his coffee, grimaces.

Nicky does the same. "That's terrible."

"Worst in town."

"Then, why?"

"Protection. Clancy's an ex-pro wrestler."

"I'd never have guessed. I took her for a tow truck."

"I wasn't ignoring you. Things have just been breaking fast on your case."

"What case? What do you mean things are breaking? How can you—"

Ryan's beeper nudges him. He looks at the message and slides out of the booth."

"Don't you dare—"

"Gotta' go. New action. I installed an intruder alarm in your apartment."

"Something I should have done myself, long ago."

"Then you'd have missed me and the best part of your life. You can come with me or wait here."

She quickly catches up to him, starts to protest the proprietary hand he places on the small of her back, pulling her along, but he's moving so swiftly she hasn't time.

* * * * * *

From the Klein's bathroom, Nicky watches Ryan use her camera to tape through the one-way mirror as Archie and Martha pace her bedroom.

"What the hell is—? "

"Shhh."

"I'm not going to shhh."

"Then I'll have to remove you. You're breaking my concentration."

"There's nothing to hear."

"I'm reading lips."

Martha dials Nicky's phone.

"Commonwealth Insurance Company."

"Who's in charge of open claims?"

"That would be our Mr. Franklin Toole. Would you like me to connect you?"

"Yes, please."

"Your name?"

"Nichole Sheridan."

CLICK

"Ms. Sheridan. I hope you're not calling to postpone your appointment."

"Appointment?"

"Yes, you're still coming at three?"

"Three?"

"You said you'd have those papers by then."

"Papers?"

"When you were here this morning, don't you remember?"

"Just a minute."

MUMBLED VOICES

Martha hands Archie the phone. "Mr. Toole, this is Mr. Fishbine, Miss Sheridan's advisor."

"Are you an attorney, Mr. Fishbine? Miss Sheridan has no need of legal counsel. All we require are a few simple questions answered."

"I'm her financial consultant."

"How may I be of help, Mr. Fishbine?"

"Help?"

"Yes, you called for a reason?"

"Oh, yeah, well, we need more time. Miss Sheridan needs more time."

"Well, when would be convenient?"

"Prob'ly a day or two. That okay?"

"Yes, of course. Can we set a time and date?"

"We'll call you, soon's things are squared around." He hangs up then gives his cell phone to Martha, tells her what to do and say. She looks down at Nicky's phone and dials that number. Her phone rings and the answering machine picks up.

"Ms. Sheridan? I'm calling for Mr. Toole. He's unable to keep his appointment with you at three this afternoon. He will contact you to reschedule."

* * * * * *

Ryan grabs Nicky's hand and pulls her to the car. As they spot the car he'd avoided earlier; Ryan slows, checks the rear-view mirror. "We've got to move quickly. Don't look back and don't lag."

They jump into the car.

"What?"

"Come up to speed. There's no time for a tutorial."

"You're saying we're being followed? By who?"

"Whom. Move, NOW!"

He jerks to a stop, reaches across, opens her door and helps her out with a gentle nudge.

A half block behind is a parked car with a dark-skinned man missing his front teeth watching from behind the wheel. Another man gets out of the car and follows her into Clancy's. Minutes later, Ryan is in a booth opposite Nicky, stirring sugar into his coffee. Nicky sips hers, screws up her eyes and winces. "Why don't we have a brandy instead?"

"Oh, her brandy will dissolve wrought-iron."

The man from the car joins his partner seated at the bar. They don't look in Ryan's direction, but see everything in the flyspecked mirror behind the bar.

Ryan whispers something to Nicky. She turns and looks to the bar.

"I told you not to look. Now they've made you."

"Ha! Not even you've done that."

"Yet!" He gets up, goes to the bar and wedges himself between the two men. "Clancy, have you lowered your standards? You never used to let patrons bring their pets."

He looks closer at the shorter of the two men. "Oh, I was wrong. It's not a pet, it's the ugliest woman on earth."

The man reaches under his arm. Ryan grabs the man's hooknose in a vise-like grip, pulls the gun from the man's shoulder holster and throws it out of reach along the bar. "Nope, I was right the first time. And it smells like it's not housebroken."

The second man pulls back his fist; Clancy reaches one hand over the bar, grabs the fist and twists. The man cringes. Clancy grins, squeezes harder. Bones snap and crunch in the man's hand. Ryan releases the reddened nose he's been wrenching and twisting.

Trying to come to the aid of his partner, the second man reaches for Clancy.

With her other hand, she grabs him by the neck and chokes until he turns blue.

"Don't nobody messes with my reg'lars."

Ryan throws a twenty on the table and pulls Nicky out the door.

CHAPTER-16
THE PAST COMES FORWARD—TO HELP OR HINDER?

Archie drives, while Martha pouts. On the radio, Frank Sinatra sings

"THE LAST DANCE."

It ends and PJ comes on. "That was for all you without a lover to cuddle up to on this cold night."

Martha shudders.

"I've said it often enough, N.S., you need to find that special someone all your own."

* * * * * *

Ryan pulls his car into traffic and Nicky stares out the car window. "I thought as a private detective you'd be able to take care of yourself."

"I am. I'm taking care of myself and you. I sometimes depend on brains, over brawn. That's why I led them here."

"I suppose you expect me to believe this wasn't a set-up?"

"Believe what you will, but I'm taking you somewhere you'll be safe."

"Sure, like your place, I suppose."

"No. I'm not sure even that's safe."

"I don't believe any of this; just take me home."

"That's not a good idea."

"Take me home or I'll get out right here."

While he's doing at least fifty, she opens the door.

"Okay, shut the door. Boy, are you ever tunnel visioned." He tunes the radio to PJ's station.

"Have you seen that sky, you night people? It's enough to make statues fall in love. Here's Lani Hall and

"SO MANY STARS."

Nicky turns it off. Ryan turns it back on.

* * * * * *

Archie parks the rental car on the shoulder of a Connecticut country road, gets out and pulls Martha into the driver's seat. Martha looks down into the dark swirling canal water.

"I'm not gonna' crash into that ditch. Look at that water."

"Not crash, gravity will ease you in and the water will break your fall."

"I don' wanna' break nothin'."

"No, you'll just tear your dress, maybe scratch your arm, lose your purse and one shoe."

"My new shoes?"

"We'll get you new ones."

"Red? Not plastic, real leather? Like that?"

"Real leather. Alligator, if you like."

"I don't think there are any red alligators."

"They dye them that color."

"Oh, right. They, like, tie 'em up first, right? I mean, cause it must be pretty hard otherwise. They prob'ly don't like it much."

"You're prob'ly right. Now, we'll come back just before commute traffic.

You'll be in the water only a few minutes before you're spotted and pulled out."

CHAPTER-17
TAKE YOUR OWN ADVICE

In the sound booth, PJ's monitor speaker plays Lani Hall. Behind her, a door

SHUTS,

a chair

SCRAPES.

PJ looks up as Eddie slides onto the seat next to her. He takes both her hands, giving her no opportunity to turn off the mike. The ON AIR light is still lit.

"Eddie what are you doing? You know I'm on the air until—"

"You always avoid serious conversation when we're alone. Here, you can't run away. PJ Blegin, I love you. You knew that already, but I want it perfectly clear and on the record so there can be no misunderstanding." He takes out a ring box. "The place might be more romantic, but there will never be a better time. Miss Pauline Blegin, will you do me the great honor of becoming my wife?"

"Eddie, you don't mean this. You haven't given it enough thought, you've—"

"You know I have. It's you avoiding the idea. Now you'll *have* to think about it. And I hope your listeners agree with me."

He puts the ring on her finger. The record ends, hits the spirals and the air goes dead.
PAUSE.

"Uh...PJ back with you. I think some Pete Fountain. Here's 'South Rampart Street Parade'."

As Pete Fountain begins, the phone lines light up the old-fashioned switchboard like a decorated Christmas tree. In her sound booth, she turns the music down and answers the first caller.

"PJ Blegin with you, caller, what's your request?"

> "I hope you appreciate what that boy went through, Miss. Blegin. My wife and I have been happily married for thirty-seven years and I still remember the difficulty I had proposing."

> "Yeah, you gonna' marry that guy?"

> "PJ you have no idea how lucky you are. My boyfriend and I have been going steady for eleven years. I thought he'd never propose. I decided not to wait any longer. After hearing you and Eddie, I just asked him. We'll be the first St. Paul's couple this June."

> "Yo, mama, sounds good.

Gwanangetjahitched.
Can I say hello to all the guys down at Froggy's Pool Hall?"

"Aren't you excited, dear? It's as romantic as a Charlotte Bronte novel."

"Miss. Blegin? My boyfriend and I were listening together. I think he's going to get up the nerve after hearing Eddie. If you say no, though, I just know he'll chicken out."

"If you expect to maintain credibility, you certainly should take your own advice about finding that one right person."

"You should answer Eddie on air, dear; we're all anxious to hear."

CHAPTER-18
SOMETIMES YOU DO IT RIGHT, BUT IT STILL GOES WRONG

Ryan pulls the Plymouth into the garage and takes Nicky's slot.

"I'll make sure it's clear. You follow in a minute."

"The garage manager will have this heap towed away before you can get back."

"Oh? What time does he come on in the morning?"

"Ha! You wish."

Ryan takes the elevator and Nicky waits. She doesn't see the man with missing teeth follow a Continental through the security gate. He opens her door and tries to slip a wire around her neck. She blocks him and drives four fingers up under his chin. He gags; his face turns white. She watches him flopping on the cement floor like a gaffed fish. When he stops moving, she feels for, but doesn't find a pulse, she uses the house intercom, calls her apartment and trembles until Ryan answers.

"Ryyyyan, come down. I just killed somebody."

"Boy, sometimes that can just ruin your whole day.

"RYAN!"

"I'm coming, Darling. Don't move anything..."

The man is breathing shallowly, his neck still red from Clancy's finger marks—her welcome to a new customer. Ryan drags him to a new Ford sedan. Using the key, he dumps him into the trunk beside a first aid kit with Klein stenciled on top.

"He tried to use this wire on you?'

"Yes, he—"

"And you defended yourself?"

"Yes."

"Where can we go where you're not known? Out of town is best."

"I'm not going anywhere until you tell me what the hell is going on."

"Okay. You stay and explain it to the cops.

She folds her arms and clenches her jaw.

He grins. "They'll have to believe you. You're a person of interest, why the ink isn't dry on your last arrest report."

"Ryan, please!"

"Do you know a safe place or not?"

She thinks, checks her purse, finds David Boyle's card and phones. "David Boyle, please. Miss Sheridan…Nicky calling." PAUSE. "David, I hope my calling isn't an inconv…" PAUSE. "Thank you, I'm glad you feel that way. I've a big favor to ask."

She turns and looks at Ryan.

"Well, it's…I need a place to stay for a few days." PAUSE. "No, the guesthouse would be fine. I have a friend with me."

She gives Ryan the Colt then drives the Plymouth while he follows in the Klein's new Ford.

* * * * * *

On a consignment car lot on Long Island, Ryan parks the Ford. In the trunk, Missing-Teeth is stirring.

Ryan opens the trunk lid. "Damn. You're still alive. Bummer. Now I'll have to off you myself."

98

"You don't scare me. You ain't gonna' hurt me."

"What makes you think that?"

"You don' wanna' go to the chair."

"The woman thinks she killed you, she was prepared to confess. I'll just let her go on thinking that way. You won't be around to dispute it."

"Most guys are just mouth when it—"

Ryan pulls the Colt, shoves it into the man's nostril. "I don't play games. You're so anxious to die you're not going to tell me who hired you, so I might as well eliminate at least one pain in the ass."

He cocks the Colt.

"I can't."

"Can't or won't?"

"Can't. I got a picture and address and five gees in a envelope, left by private messenger. I checked. Sometimes I can like, you know, get more later if I know who."

"Blackmail."

"Private enterprise. Hey, lemme outta' here. I gotta take a crap."

"Go ahead. It won't bother me, it's not my car. They'll have you in the slammer before you get to tell them anything. And once you do, I'll have no more trouble from you. The man who hired you will teach you to swim holding an anchor."

"Hey, man."

"Make all the noise you want. Security guards check every hour. If you're still here in the morning. I'll decide what to do with you."

Ryan slams the trunk lid. takes a $26,000 FIRM sign from the windshield of a late model Corvette and places it on the Klein's windshield, then climbs into the Plymouth.

"What did you—?"

"I'll deal with him later."

* * * * * *

They enter the double-gated and quarter-mile driveway of the Boyle Estate.

"Who lives here, the Rockefellers?"

"No, my boy friend."

As they park beside a six-car garage adjacent a guest cottage, David greets them and sees Ryan for the first time. Leading them to the drawing room where a maid and butler wait to serve champagne, caviar, and canapés, he says, "Cook has gone to bed, but if you're hungry I'll get him up."

"David, this is Mr. York."

David frowns, "When you said a friend, naturally I thought..."

Ryan sees the adoration in the boy's eyes when he looks at Nicky, and says, "Don't worry; I'm not sure I really qualify as a friend."

Nicky steps between them and says, "You don't."

"No, I can see it." The boy shakes his head. "You're already more than that."

She responds with, "Frankly, you couldn't be further from the truth."

To Ryan, the boy says, "I haven't a chance with her anymore, have I?"

"I don't know; when this is over, we can flip a coin for her."

They both look to Nicky. "Gee guys, you don't know how flattering this is for me to hear."

David ponders, "I'm better at squash or chess.

100

There's time enough after I've heard what trouble you're in, but I don't expect I'll get much truth tonight. We'll talk in the morning, over breakfast."

* * * * * *

Back in Connecticut, Martha climbs atop the door as the current carries the car to the center of the rapidly flowing irrigation canal. Passing motorists drive on without slowing. She's below their line of sight.

CHAPTER-19
"FOR ALL WE KNOW"

The Boyle guesthouse is nicer than a $2,000 a night hotel suite Ryan checks the window and door locks. Nicky follows as he talks. "Commonwealth hired me to trace a woman who disappeared over twenty years ago. I learned that she'd had a baby girl seven months after leaving her husband."

"Wait, you're saying my parents were married? Naturally I thought—"

"They met when your mother was Quebec Mardi-Gras Parade Queen and your father Pageant Chairman."

"Tell me more about them."

"Yvette was French-Canadian of simple background. Jerome was a speculator. His family had lost great wealth during the '29 Depression. He maintained the champagne taste with then a beer budget."

Ryan enters the bedroom and strips to his shorts. She's inches behind. "Because his family would never have accepted her, they married secretly and combined a honeymoon in Louisiana while checking his oil leases. She'd had enough of the cold. On the way back up north, she said if he loved her they'd have stayed in the south."

He turns down the covers on both sides of the bed. "He refused and when they reached Buffalo, she left him after a final argument."

"He assumed she'd returned to the south and sent detectives to New Orleans to find her. That was a mistake. She'd stayed in Buffalo.

Then, when she learned she was pregnant, she moved to New York City."

He gets into bed. She takes one pillow and the spread over to the armchair.

"You were born and three years later, when she learned she had an aneurysm, she left you with the Sisters. That was the end of it."

"The end of it? You started your campaign of terror against me. Why?"

"What do you mean terror? I never used force or intimidation. Never asked you to do anything."

He reaches over and turns out the bedside light.

In the dark, she undresses as far as her under garments and says, "You lied, schemed, contrived, falsified."

He doesn't answer and she hears only his even breathing. She moves to the other side of the bed and leans over him. "Ryan, don't you dare go to sleep."

She shakes him but only results in allowing him to pull her into bed with him. He holds her so tightly that squirming is useless. She has no karate counter for this; and besides she's exhausted.

In the pre-dawn light, Ryan, hearing her come from the bathroom, forces his eyes open. She's dressed and still staring daggers.

He sits up. "I see you're still annoyed about that *fantasy* business."

"You took advantage of my weakness."

"Oh nonsense. I staged a little production that you've probably often created all by yourself."

"Possibly, but not with <u>you</u> as white knight."

"Of course not. You didn't know me and couldn't dream about me until you did."

"But—"

"Besides, I don't think you have any weaknesses."

"You still haven't told me why."

"I promised what, not why."

She starts out. He grabs her and pulls her down onto the bed. She twists out of his grip, bends his head backward and chops the side of his neck. He moans and his eyes roll back in his head.

"Oh my God. Ryan, what have I done?" She lets go of the hold and shakes him. "Oh darling, I held back, I didn't mean to—"

He grips her wrists and kisses her. She resists, but only weakly.

"You almost gave me the shaken baby syndrome."

With purse, car keys and earrings in hand, she says, "You've given me a lot to think about. I need time to digest it." She slips out, and in the driving rain, leaves in the Plymouth.

Nicky lets herself into PJ's apartment, undresses and leaves her earrings on the bureau. She showers, puts on a chenille robe and slippers. Frowning, she takes aspirin and lies atop the bed and tries to sort lies from truth.

* * * * * *

From a weather-beaten pick-up, a farmer throws Martha a line.

As she reaches for it with numb fingers, she slips into the rushing water and is sucked under.

CHAPTER-20
RECONNECTING

Just after dawn, Ryan knocks at PJ's apartment. There's no answer, so he starts to pick the lock.

"Get away, or I'll call the police."

"Go ahead, that way at least I'll know you're safe."

The door opens. Half-heartedly she tries to hold him back, but he enters, hangs up his wet coat and looks her up and down. She's left her clothes to dry on bathroom towel racks and is wearing one of PJ's crazy outfits.

"You can't...wait. How did you get here? I took your car."

"David loaned me the Bugatti."

"Now! The why!"

He pours two cups of coffee, hands her one. "When I started, I did a lot of in-depth research. This started as just a job, then as professional position. But, what I learned made me take a personal interest."

"You mean by terrorizing me?"

He pulls her down beside him. "Oh, please. Even that first time, you weren't terrorized"

She refuses to look at him directly.

"Then, I became intrigued by your ability to adapt."

"By that, you mean gullibility."

He finds the bathroom, strips and showers. She stands at the bathroom door and holds out a clean towel for him.

"Kind of, but that made the plan possible. I had to know you were unflappable."

She grins. "Well, I was intrigued by your imagination and resourcefulness. But what did you hope to gain? Once the insurance company made contact it was all over."

When he comes out and dries off, he watches her eyes reveal the machinations of her mind. She's so focused, he has no trouble pulling her onto his lap and kissing her. With a fresh towel, she dries his hair.

"An event I was trying very hard to postpone. But you didn't ask why I had to know you were unflappable."

"Okay, I'm asking it now."

"Because when the hard part comes, you might have cracked under the pressure."

"Wait, you're saying there's more strife to come?"

"Well, you could call it strife. Someone is trying to kill you and that's just the fun part."

She shakes her head. "Hopefully, once I have this all processed, it will make sense. But if that's true, why are you involved?"

"Because I fell in love when all I had was your picture. I had to give you the time you needed."

Now she has to look into his eyes. "To what, fall in love with you?"

"Of course."

"That's ridiculous. Nobody falls in love with a picture."

"Dana Andrews fell in love with Gene Tierney's portrait and he thought she was dead at the time. I knew you were alive."

"That's the movies; this is real life."

He holds her head with the towel and kisses her, twice. "Life imitates art. Besides, it must be love. You even look sexy to me in your Hee Haw outfit."

They glare at each other. He pulls her onto the bed and they wrestle a while. Both tire and fall asleep atop the bed.

Later that morning, Ryan wakes first, covers Nicky and shaves with a miniature Lady Schick. Nicky wakes and dresses. She almost leaves without her pearl earrings. He holds them out to her. "Don't forget these."

With an angry swipe, she grabs them from his hand. "I still don't believe you. You made it all up to get your hands on the money."

"What money? You don't even know what's at stake here."

"It has to be a lot for you to go through all this trouble."

"If that's the case, marry me and I'll sign a pre-nup."

"You're crazy."

"Crazy about you."

"You're just trying to squeeze out of this."

"Watch Dr. Phil. The man is the one always portrayed as afraid of commitment. Bossing men around for so long, you've developed a gender crisis and crossed the line. But I'm bringing you back. I've expressed my love for you, but you haven't reciprocated."

Not having a response ready, she heads for the door.

"Where do you think you're going?"

"I'll probably see you around. You're not going to tell me the whole truth, so I'll just be moseying along."

"Can't mosey now. If you want the whole truth, we'll have to go to Miami."

"What?"

"Miami, it's in Florida, a place for sun and fun."

"But why are we going?"

"You mean besides the sun and fun? I'd tell you, but you wouldn't believe me. I have to show you."

CHAPTER-21
TAKING OUT THE GARBAGE

From Kennedy Airport, Ryan phones. "Rockport police? It won't do any good to trace this call. We left a thief in the trunk of the car he was trying to steal from the U-Sell Lot near the train station." PAUSE. "Oh, we're the Avenging Angels." PAUSE. "Well, you've heard of us now." He hangs up.

From an opposite corner, Nicky phones and gets PJ's answering machine. "Peej, I'd hoped to catch you. There's so much to tell you. That Ryan York? You gave me his card; remember? Well, he's been coming into my room late at night… anyway, it all had to do with his finding out that I'm an heiress and there are people trying to kill us. One of us at least, I'm not sure yet just which. Oh, we used your apartment, might have left it a mess."

Ryan grabs her and they run to the departure gate, are the last to board the plane.

The first class South Air stewardess serves them champagne. Nicky tries to refuse. Ryan hands her his glass, gets another for himself then stares at her until she takes a sip. "Miami is where I recommended the detective, Archie Fishbine, to find your look-alike. He found Martha."

"They're the ones in my apartment? What were they doing there?"

"Planning a story for the insurance company. They had to shift gears when they learned you were alive."

"Why would they think I wasn't alive?"

"Because I told Archie you'd drowned in a boating accident outside Miami."

"Why go so far for a P.I.?"

"Because Archie is the most corrupt sleaze bag I could find. And besides, anyone local might have stumbled onto the truth."

"Why would they try fooling an insurance company?"

"For the multi-million dollar policy."

"Wait a minute. How could they <u>expect</u> to fool an insurance company?"

"Because I promised the insurance company to supply documentation that proved you were who I said you were and were entitled to the money."

"And my look-alike was going to secure herself as heir. But why would you promise that?"

"Because they paid me a fifty thousand dollar bonus to either find you or prove you were dead."

"Suppose this Archie dug into your drowning woman story?"

"Not a story; Annette St. Ettienne was lost at sea. She was an orphan of the right age, look, background, blood type and ethnic sub-classification.

"But there would still be some trace."

"No. I destroyed all physical evidence and official reports. You think I'd make the same mistake as Tricky Dicky?"

"No, but—"

"It took me three months to find her. After I proved it was you, I spent another month to wipe out all traces of her existence."

"Why...?"

He kisses her, holds out two glasses for the stewardess to refill. "The rest comes on the return flight. Sit back and enjoy my company. After we land I'll brief you on what we have to do there."

Nicky sees her reflection in the window. It keeps changing to various look-a-likes. Then it fades to a fantasy scene—A wide river amidst a jungle setting. Ryan is tied to a stake. She drives off circling, man-hungry woman warriors, then unties him and throws him into the river. Crocodiles slide into the water, heading for their dinner. She smiles, obviously deciding fantasies aren't all bad, sips champagne and closes her eyes.

In the next fantasy, she's dressed in a white strapless pearl-covered wedding dress that's so short her legs look five feet long. Kneeling at her side, Ryan, in a tattered and torn tux, holds his handcuffed wrists up in a begging attitude. She smiles even wider.

* * * * * *

Rockport Police open the Ford trunk, hold their noses and arrest Missing Front Teeth. He's shivering, his teeth chattering, and he's sobbing too much to give any rational answers to their questions. He does, however admit that was about to steal another car. He wasn't too discombobulated to want to deal with the stone cold killer who put him in the trunk and may come back. Not wanting to put him into their clean patrol car, the police call for a riot-wagon to come for him.

* * * * * *

Connecticut emergency vehicles line the edge of the road, as Martha is loaded into an ambulance to be transported to New York. Archie is in attendance.

* * * * * *

At the Miami Airport, Ryan hails a cab, holds the door for Nicky. "Any inexpensive dress shop downtown."

He selects the right outfit for her. Coming from a Modern Woman chain shop, she wears a tight orange dress, red pumps and huge neon-pink plastic earrings. Next he takes her to a five-and-ten, gets a ghetto blaster and a plastic leopard-print purse, stuffing it with cheap perfume and bubble gum.

At a hair and nail salon, he looks at the photo of Martha again, decides to leave the hair alone.

"Just the nails; how long will that take?"

"'Pends on whatcha' want."

He points to a chart. "I think this. With lots of glitter."

"Good choice, my boy friend likes me to wear that when we go the dog races. He says, 'no flash no cash'."

"Then I'm sure it will be right." The manicurist smiles in return for the compliment.

At Palmetto Court, Ryan lets Nicky out of the taxi. He waits, watching her pick her way up the broken pavement in the too-tight dress and too-high heels, swinging her gaudy purse and snapping bubble gum.

The ghetto blaster on her shoulder plays rap music at full volume. She knocks, smiles at the landlady. "Listen, you can have my old stuff. I'm moving out of this dump."

"What about the back rent you owe?"

"Try and get it. I'll be a thousand miles away and rich enough to pay a knee buster to keep people like you from botherin' me."

She sashays her way back to the waiting cab. Ryan holds the door open for her. "Still not enough hip action."

CHAPTER-22
IN THE HOSPITAL, IT'S ALL GOOD

Martha is wheeled into room 207 and a medical team hovers over her.

"Where am I?"

"Parkview Hospital, Manhattan. You've had an accident, but you're going to be fine. Try and get some rest."

Archie follows the doctor into the hallway. "What's wrong with her, doc?"

"She has hysterical amnesia. Probably from the concussion when she hit the concrete abutment. Now I don't want you to worry."

"How long will it last?"

"There's no telling."

"I talked to her on the way in, but she couldn't remember any insurance policy, my name, nothing of the past."

"That's not unusual."

Archie turns his head and secretly smiles. "That's just great."

* * * * * *

At Bowlarama, Ryan waits in the taxi as Nicky climbs out. He stops her, reaches out and unfastens the top two buttons of her dress. She's greeted by whistles and catcalls from a bowling league waiting for drinks.

"Hey, Martha, where the hell you been?"

"Yeah, we been so lonesome lately we even went home to our old ladies."

"Not me, I'd rather slap the chicken."

117

She waves, selects acid rock from the jukebox and as the screeching noise builds, approaches the bar.

The bartender smiles,"Glad yer back, doll; our business is in the crapper since you left."

"I'm scammin' millions from some jerk in New York so I don't need all you little people anymore."

"Listen, bitch, I paid you an advance before you left, and what about your uniform deposit?"

"Use it for the next round heel comes lookin' for a job."

She blows a bubble that pops and smears her lipstick. She flounces her way back out to the cab.

Ryan opens the door for her. "I thought you were going to blow it. Walking and chewing gum at the same time. But you didn't falter once. I'm so proud of you."

* * * * * *

Aboard Sunbelt Airlines on the return trip, Nicky, dressed and acting like herself again, looks into the window and sees reflected:

> *Herself at the age of 11. She meets PJ and they immediately become fast friends.*
> *At 13, She and PJ receive Christmas presents from Sister Elizabeth.*
> *At 14, They both feel the changes of fast-approaching womanhood.*
> *At 15, She and PJ, ski in non-Nun-approved outfits that reveal lush bodies in full bloom.*

118

At 16, Sister Elizabeth watches as she crashes the nun's old Ford against a racetrack wall.
At 17, She and PJ attend a dance and are surrounded by boys.
At 18, PJ, on-stage sings while Nicky photographs her. Sister Elizabeth, serving punch, smiles proudly.

Nicky and Ryan deplane at LaGuardia Airport, and enter a waiting cab. Ryan says, "Broadway and 42nd."

Surprised, Nicky stares at him. "Only things around there now are porn shops. You need stimulation?"

"I can't seem to get enough, since you took me to that XXX-rated motel."

The driver looks up, readjusts the mirror to focus on Nicky, then slows at 42nd.

A flashy blonde smiles enticingly and Roxie swings a flaking gold *lamĕ* purse on a brass chain.

"Stop here." At the curb, Ryan rolls down the window and asks the blonde, "How much for the night?"

"Century note."

To Roxie, "How about you?"

"A grand."

He opens the door and says to Roxie, "Okay, get in."

The blonde watches in shock. "Uh, hey, I could charge more, make it a special party rate like maybe for the three of ..." She sees Nicky... "The four of us....?"

"Maybe next time." To the driver, "Calcutta Arms."

The driver turns and says, "You're on some kinda expense account, huh, buddy? And mega vitamins?" He looks at Roxie. "But they won't help if yer eyesight is goin'."

The cab pulls into traffic. The driver readjusts his mirror to inspect Roxie. He shakes his head, fixes his mirror again on Nicky and leaves it there.

"Nicky, this is Roxie. You two have a lot in common. You're both crazy about me, but I don't want you fighting over me. What's shakin,' Rox?"

"He's still in his office, usually works 'til six. The others have made their move. Martha's in the hospital and Archie's contacted the insurance company."

"I didn't think they'd dare, now."

"But they figure you've been scared off or else this will flush you and they'd get a clear shot at you."

"They've really gone over the edge."

"We knew they would, with what's at stake."

Ryan shakes his head. "But, not so fast."

"Boss, you taught me never to underestimate a foe. The girl's in Parkview, room 207."

"How bad and how?"

"Scratches and faked amnesia. It's how they'll cover anything they don't know. She just can't remember. Your file proves she's the real McCoy. Commonwealth wants to clear their books. They have to pay and the beneficiary matters little to them."

"I did create a solid case."

Nicky grows increasingly irritated. "Are you ever going to tell me what is going on?"

"Rox is a P.I. I hired to keep track of things."

"And to record the evidence and leave the fraud plan with an attorney. To cover us against any kickback."

"But, Boss, are you sure that and our Miami snafu will be enough to bust them?"

"No, but, anything more would be dangerous."

Nicky frowns and says, "We'll go to David's and I'll tell you how we'll work it. We have to return his car anyway."

She gives directions to PJ's apartment.

CHAPTER-23
THANK GOODNESS ALL THE EXCITEMENT IS OVER

At David's, Nicky and Roxie fill their plates from an elaborate buffet.

Ryan drinks black coffee, looks anxious. He frowns and says to Nicky, "Shouldn't we wait until you're sure PJ will go along with this?"

"She'll do it. She's always complaining that there's not enough excitement in her life."

David smiles and dials the phone. "Admitting, please. PAUSE. Admitting? This is David Boyle." PAUSE. "Of course, THAT David Boyle. I'm on your board of directors, Miss...?" PAUSE. "Miss Parnell. I rely on your discretion. A friend has need of quiet bed rest. The Betty Ford Clinic offers little privacy for anyone high profile." PAUSE. "Yes, you understand. She will be admitted as Agnes Smith and attended by her own physician and nurse. She must have room 209. Her chart calls it her lucky number. Silly, I'm sure, but, you know how the *nouveau riche* are."

Ryan nervously spills coffee down his shirt.

In the Parkview lot, Ryan parks the limo. Roxie and Nicky are dressed in traditional black and white nun's habits with only their scrubbed faces showing. Roxie goes to the main entrance and watches. As Nicky waits, Ryan slides his arm around her waist and lays a most un-parochial kiss on her.

Less then twenty minutes later, PJ arrives in a conservative (for her) dark blue dress and white faux fur jacket. She wears a white glove on her left hand and carries the right glove.

Ryan jumps from the Limo and makes it to the front door just as PJ reaches the reception desk.

"Miss Nicole Sheridan, please."

The Candy Striper looks for the room number on her chart.

"I'm sorry, this yellow tag means no visitors."

"What else does the doctor say about her condition?"

"I'm afraid you'll have to speak with Mister Fishbine, he's her advisor and an old friend."

"WHAT? Where are the phones?"

The Candy Striper points to an alcove beside the front entrance. She heads that way.

Ryan takes a converging course. "Miss Blegen? PJ? Nicky and I have been trying to reach you. Would you come with me, please?"

"I'm afraid I don't know you and I'm not going anywhere with some stranger."

"We called you from David's place on Long Island. I trust she told you about David? She's outside in the limo. You can stand in the front entrance. I'll get her to wave. I hope you haven't made contact with Mr. Fishbine yet."

She shakes her head and he dashes off to the car. Nicky rolls the window down. PJ watches, but in the nun's costume and at that distance, nobody would recognize their own mother.

Ryan returns to the entrance, notices PJ's hesitation and realizes he must do something to close ranks.

"Does that glove cover an engagement ring? Until you and Eddie can make an official announcement? I don't know what more I can say, unless, perhaps, I mention spending the night with Nicky in your spare bedroom?"

"You and Nicky in my...?"

"That dusty rose is such a warm color and it goes so well with the brass bed. Normally I don't care for modern furniture, but..."

PJ takes his arm and drags him toward the hospital cafeteria. "Tell me while I eat. Lately, I've developed a taste for baseball hotdogs."

Dressed as an M.D., Ryan checks PJ in. He carries Nicky's clothes bag. The two fake nuns follow them to 209.

In room 207 Ryan inspects Martha from head to foot. Using his cell phone, he photographs her with her eyes closed.

Switching the nun's outfit with PJ, Nicky, in 209, lies uncomfortably in bed, puts her pearl earrings on the nightstand. PJ sets the video camera on the tripod as Ryan enters from the connecting bathroom. Bandaging Nicky exactly as Martha, he grins. "You know, naked, she only looks like you from the neck up." Nicky throws a pillow at him. "There's one more thing. I told you I recommended Archie. I let you assume the insurance company hired him. They didn't, I did. You have an uncle who gains nothing if you're found dead <u>before</u> inheriting. If <u>after</u>, he gets everything." A beeper goes off on his belt. "Oops, gotta go."

"Ryan, you come back here. RYAN!" She reaches for another pillow, but it's too late, he's gone. She dials her phone."

* * * * * *

Captain Bowden, N.Y.P.D., holds the phone to his ear, listens and writes on a pad—Sheridan, N., Parkview 207, fraud, murder attempt, multi-million...

* * * * * *

A white-smocked intern shows Uncle Ben (the man from the white apartment and the subject of Roxie's surveillance) to 207 and leaves. From the connecting bathroom, PJ videos him as he updates his plan to cheat his niece of her inheritance.

Ryan meets Capt. Bowden in the lobby and hands him a file, then he inserts a DVD into a portable player. It shows Nicky, swathed in bandages in a hospital bed with just enough of her face showing to be clearly identifiable. "I've signed a complete confession. This file and video explain how my partner, Archie, and I, planned and implemented an insurance fraud."

The Captain says, "Let me go over this material before I make any arrests. I want to be able to form proper questions."

Ryan backs away. "I must get back to my patient. Join us in 207 when you're ready."

In 209, Nicky changes back into the nun's habit and leaves.

In 207, police, led by Capt. Bowden, surround the bed and confront Martha.

"I don't know what the hell you're talking about. I never made no damn confession."

In the excitement, nobody notices that Uncle Ben, the mastermind of the scam is missing.

As Archie and Martha are led out in cuffs, Nicky and Roxie, dressed as nuns, hold St. Therese Orphanage donation cans. Archie stares at Nicky, turns his attention to Roxie. They're familiar, he's seen them somewhere before, but can't place them.

Captain Bowden tells an officer to secure the suspects into the back seat. "I'll bring down the evidence."

CHAPTER-24
OKAY, SO WE WERE WRONG ABOUT HOSPITAL SAFETY

Back in 207, a nurse flirts with "Dr." Ryan, while in the adjoining bathroom, Uncle Ben has heard everything. He comes out holding a .25 automatic on Ryan and PJ, takes Ryan's keys, wallet, pager and a beeper from the nightstand. The only person he wants and doesn't have is Nichole.

"Where is she?" He demands of Ryan.

"I don't know."

"I'll kill you if I have to. I've gone too far to stop now."

"You're stopped already."

"Not if I dispose of her in time."

"And the phony one? You'll have to kill her too."

"It's a big ocean and I only need one body."

"And you think I'm going to help you with that?"

"You were well paid."

"To find her. I did."

"But, you led me to Fishbine. You said she was killed in Miami waters."

"That was to keep you from finding her yourself."

"There's enough for us both. I'll give you a third."

"You want to involve me in embezzlement and the murder of your own niece for only 33 percent? You're a cheapskate. You won't even split 50/50, when I'm the only one who can make it all work."

"All right, an even division. Where is she? There isn't much time."

"Even less time than you think. No, not even for all of it."

"You're crazy; I'll drag you into it with me."

"You can try."

"I'll..." He looks at Ryan's beeper. He turns it on. A red light makes a clicking sound.

Ryan blanches. "That's not..."

"Turn around."

"No. I figure I can take at least four slugs from that thing. Enough time for me to twist your pencil neck 360 degrees."

"I'll kill this nurse first."

"If you do, I'll have plenty of time to take it away from you and I won't have to take any slugs."

A nurse's assistant opens the door, bumping into Ryan. It gives Ben enough time to pull PJ in front of him. Ryan is unable to get to him before he kills a very frightened PJ.

Ben tells the nurse's assistant to tie Ryan's hands behind his back with I.V. tubing, then forces them ahead of him. He follows the clicking to Nicky's earrings on the nightstand of 209 and turns the gun back onto PJ. "Where is she?"

"Who?"

"You know who. The woman assigned to this room."

Thinking fast, PJ says, "I'm just here for a little pre-engagement party." Proudly she shows him her engagement ring. "Try next door. There was a lot of commotion from there not long ago."

Ben hears voices next door. He shoves his captives through the interconnecting bathroom. PJ points to Ben's gun and steps out of the way. When he looks up, he's staring at Captain Bowden and two other officers. They all pull their guns. It's not a Mexican Standoff. It's at least three 38 Specials vs one .25, that's 114 to 25.

One uniformed officer cuffs Ben.   Another unties "Dr. York."

* * * * * *

Just after dawn, in Nicky's apartment, both sides of her bed are rumpled. Nicky is on one side, the other side is empty. Propped up with pillows, she's absorbed reading her file.

Ryan comes from the bathroom, his face lathered. "Your houseboy should be back soon."

"Umm."

He dresses. "I've a few ends to clean up. I'll see you back here later?"

"Ah huh."

He kisses her, but gets a less than satisfactory response, as she can't take her eyes from the file.

He leaves and she looks out the window, staring fixed-focus at nothing.

To herself she mouths,

The Williams family made a fortune on Canadian beer, switching to gin during prohibition. They made another fortune selling uniforms to the army during WWII. After the war Jerome went into commodities.

Ben branched into women's fashion designs. He went broke twice. Jerome saved him both times.

She looks back at the photographs. In one she's 13, in the next she's 16, and the third is the studio pose from Ryan's desk then sees something she'd missed. Sitting bolt upright, she studies the 13-year-old.

CHAPTER-25
TYING UP THE LOOSE ENDS

Nicky enters Franklin Toole's office accompanied by Marion-a tall, slender young man. Sister Elizabeth and a well-dressed man, James, are already seated. Toole makes the introductions. "Ms. Sheridan, James Meredith, the bank-appointed conservator."

She shakes his hand and smiles at a bewildered-looking Sister Elizabeth.

"Miss Sheridan, Sister Elizabeth has explained that documentation was destroyed in the '75 fire. Since your fingerprints and dental records have also been destroyed, we have based acceptance of you as legal heir on Mr. York's investigation, but we can't cut the check until Thursday."

Nicky says, "I think I can make things easier. This is my attorney, Marion Webster."

He shoots his cuffs and says in a patronizing tone, "I've been retained to see that Miss Sheridan's wishes are carried out in all details and specifications."

James Meredith, adds, "Based on the insurance company's acceptance, I'm prepared to settle the entire estate on Miss Sheridan."

They all look to Marion. He takes papers from his briefcase and, applying wire-rimmed bifocals, starts to read.

The door

SLAMS

open and an out-of-breath Ryan enters.

"Are all your damn elevators stuck at the roof? I had to climb the stairs. Did I miss anything?"

Nicky glowers at him and the others ignore him.

Marion continues, "Miss Sheridan has instructed me to forfeit her entire inheritance and see that it's directed to the St. Therese Orphanage. Per the Joe Lewis precedent, all taxes are avoided by direct transfer of all proceeds to a non-revocable trust. The three million insurance brings the estate value to over 15 million. Sister Elizabeth, as trustee, may access it directly or she may choose only the two and a half million annual interest."

Sister Elizabeth faints. Luckily, Toole keeps smelling salts handy and Ryan catches her in strong arms. She comes to looking into his smiling eyes.

* * * * * *

Later that same day, Ryan knocks at the Boyle Mansion. The butler opens and says in a haughty voice. "I was to inform you that neither Master David nor Miss Sheridan wish to extend hospitality unto you."

"Tell them I'll huff and I'll puff and I'll blow their damn house down."

"I shall give them your message. IF...you would be so kind as to remove your foot from the door."

136

Moments later, David opens the door. "Nicky said 'we should let you blow your brains out.' I said that would take forever since this house is reinforced brick, not straw or sticks. She said, 'even better. You'd come down the chimney, so we should catch you in a pot of boiling oil'."

"And what did you say?"

"I told her to take you to the guest house and straighten it out between you. Come in and get her. You're lucky, if I hadn't an international billion dollar exchange to verify, I'd give you a run for your money."

Ryan nods, "I can only thank my Guardian Angel for not forcing me to go head to head with you. I'm sure I'd lose."

"You're overselling it, but you'd better treat her right or I'll tromp on you like an <u>Avenging</u> Angel."

Ryan follows him into the library where Nicky sits with untouched finger sandwiches and champagne. Gabrielle, a lovely woman of about twenty-one, enters, waving papers. In a pronounced French accent, "Msgr David, you have make the mistake with conjugal the verbs, yes?"

David sighs, looks to Ryan. "Some think having a live-in tutor is easy. If you'll excuse me, I must get on with my lesson."

Gabrielle leads him out, but at the doorway he turns to Ryan, "You <u>will</u> let me know how it all turns out? If she is <u>seriously</u> rejecting you, my offer to her stands."

Ryan follows Nicky around the guesthouse as she straightens things. "You really gave it all away?"

"Yep. We're both out of work. How much have you saved?"

"About a hundred and sixty grand."

"I've about three hundred thousand in savings and over two hundred thousand in C.D.'S."

He pulls her down onto the couch and carefully watches her eyes for a tell. "What tipped you?"

"The photos. The 13 year old had pierced ears. I had mine done at 16. So the real heiress drowned off Miami? Who does that make me? Annette?"

"The Sisters named you Nicole Sheridan; there's no reason to change that. I thought this was more appealing than learning that your mother was a kindergarten schoolteacher, your father a dentist from Idaho. When they were both killed in a river rafting accident in upstate, you were placed with St. Therese temporarily, then all your records fell through the cracks."

SILENCE

"The money?"

"Annette was dead and I figured you could use it."

"But Ben could only gain upon my death after I'd taken the money?"

"That was next on his agenda. He had to put you in the ground before you could make a will excluding him. It's why I had to do it this way, to see that he stays in jail."

"How long have you been two-timing me with Roxie? Never mind, I forgive you."

138

She takes his car keys and pushes him out the door. "We can talk on the way."

CHAPTER-26
WHAT? YOU MEAN THERE'S MORE?

Ryan squirms on the broken springs of the passenger seat of the Plymouth, his eyes closed. "I don't guess David would let us use that snazzy dark blue two-seater in the garage."

"Oh, no, now that I'm unemployed and nearly broke, I wouldn't feel right reaching above my station. A vintage Plymouth is all that I deserve." She starts the engine and moves the car along the waterside park where joggers pass, families eat picnic lunches, kids and dogs play with Frisbees. "I can sell cars, produce TV commercials, teach tennis or swimming, maybe write a book about giving away fifteen million dollars. Why do I need you?"

"You want me."

"Even if that's true, my pride demands more. I'd have to want something only you could offer. What were you before you became a snooper?"

"I was in the Navy."

"And you did what in the Navy, besides seducing female swabbies?"

"Underwater demolition, mine sweeping and metal detecting."

"Underwater mine sweeping?"

"Yes, why?"

"Metal detecting underwater?"

"Yeah, some mines got away and drifted. We had to chase them across the Indian Ocean."

"They're small, right? I mean bigger than a breadbox, smaller than a compact car?"

They pass the Rockport Yacht Club. A square-rigger is on display.

"Well, sure, but..."

"We could start a salvage operation. There are lots of commercial wrecks. They recently found a German U-boat right outside New York Harbor. Then there's the Oak Isle Treasure."

"That's chasing rainbows."

"Something I've done all my life. Of course you'd have to teach me to snorkel, dive, that sort of thing?"

"Well, yeah, but..."

"A small boat; one bunk. We'd have to get cozy. Three years should determine whether we could make it work as partners."

"In everything?"

She shakes her head. "Well, yes except you'll have to give up the silly idea that you're my equal."

Ryan pulls the keys from the ignition and jumps out. As the car coasts to the curb and stops, unlocks the trunk and removes two costume-rental metal swords. He throws one to Nicky. She grabs it, assumes the fencer's stance. They skirmish; clash swords.

Passing motorists and joggers stop to watch.

Ryan calls out in a loud voice, "Hold, Norman wench. Thinkest thou to couple with a Saxon man on good Saxon soil as an equal?"

"Ha! Be I Norman, I be more than thou deserveth, nay, more than _any_ commoner can handle. But, thou be wrong; my blood is as loyal to Richard as you lay claim."

"Say on, wench."

"_Say_? Nay, I'll do more. I'll _lay_ on with my blade."

142

"Lay on then, if bloodletting be thine only passion."

In seconds, the crowd has grown to over a hundred. All are perhaps convinced their seeing part of a play or a movie.

"Nay, lad. Neither mine only passion, nor even my favorite."

"Say what then, wench. I shall do my best to accommodate thee."

"Thou <u>shalt</u> accommodate a cold bed, lest thou put aside calling me wench."

"What wouldst thou that I call thee? For in truth thou art a saucy wench."

"Call me…If thou wouldst call and have me come, Mistress. But, hear this, I shall never call thee master."

She disarms him, holds her sword to his throat in the classic manner.

"Nor ever did I expect such, but better I call thee missus."

"After a fortnight of coupling, we shall talk more on it. We should know better, then, if our humors truly doth properly flow together."

"That then is your last word on it, mistress?"

"Be not misled. Whether it be that or another, know this. I *shall* have the last word."

"Done!"

She jabs her blade into the ground, holds out her hand for him to shake. Instead, he pulls her into his arms, lays her back and kisses her. The audience cheers. Under her breath, she mumbles, "Easy sailor. My partner gets jealous when I'm on the beach. And my boyfriend David is <u>always</u> jealous."

He tries to hold her, but she pushes him away and says, "You'd have been harder to handle if you'd known that you had me at…"

"You can't get anything worthwhile by running from it."

Let her know who's boss from the very beginning; then continue thinking it's you.

AFTERWORD

Proof reading and rewriting as many times as it takes is like restoring an abandoned and abused Duesenberg. You don't want to show it before you've removed any rust, replaced broken parts and dressed her in new paint.

INTRODUCTION

Please allow me to share the following with you. Remember; positive word of mouth is the best form of advertisement. You may order all from Amazon.com.

13-An Hour's Pleasure

16-A Taste of Money

19-A Torch Unseen

21-Black Kat

12-Cold Fire

7-Fantasy Impromptu

3-Fools Rush In

6-Greene's Field

9-Houston, We Have A Problem

2-Independence

17-Just For Kids

4-Just Passin' Thru

1-Liberty

11-Naked We Came

8-Nature Abhors a Vacuum

22-Night Train and Country Gravy

18-One Fist is Iron

20-September 17th

10-Shallow Water

14-The Angel and The Eighteen Wheeler

23-The Big E

15-'37 Indian

5-Writer's Block

ALL my books is good. Some is even GOODER.

EXCERPT NATURE ABHORS A VACUUM 12-15-14

CHAPTER-1
YOU DON'T NEED TO BE IN A HOT, DIRTY, SMELLY, NOISY ENGINE TO DRIVE A TRAIN

Between the cluster of tall buildings and through a blanket of early morning fog that lies just above the third floor level; as if to allow San Franciscans an extra fifteen minutes of sleep before facing the stress of another day. Brandon, 35, lean, bookish type, jogging, nearly stumbles over a sleeping form and her shopping cart with one yellow wheel in the Post Office street level doorway. A full orchestra is heard, as if filtered through curtains. He pulls off the ear buds and before he turns off his CD player, Mendelssohn's

"MIDSUMMER NIGHT'S DREAM"

Spills into the early morning air. He takes the escalator to the second floor (Arcade level) and crosses the bridge way to GOLDEN GATEWAY building #3 and his split-level condo. #207. The Ferry Building clock reads 6:01.

Showered, Brandon can see the street through his living room window. The form and yellow-wheeled shopping cart are gone. His condo is decorated in an eclectic combination of Scandinavian modern furniture, New Zealand and Scottish ethnic artifacts, fencing foils, high-tech, detailed drawings of aircraft, autos, and a ¼ scale remote controlled red model XK Jag and a tripod-mounted telescope. The entire apartment is studiously and meticulously neat and orderly.

By the Ferry Building clock, it's 6:47. At the Starbrite Restaurant's outdoor patio table, a waiter brings Brandon oatmeal, OJ and black coffee. Brandon helps an old man, who seems lost, to an adjacent table. "Is this gentleman bothering you, Mr. Harriman?"

"No, Charles. He's an often-confused neighbor who used to play sax with Duke Ellington and Fats Waller. Bring him breakfast and put it on my tab. To the old man, "Have your breakfast, Mr. Blakely, and remember you're #206, I'm #207."

By 7:47, Brandon is in his office, only a hundred yard and a five-minute walk from his condo. He winds the Howard Railroad Station pendulum clock and takes mail from his secretary, Claire Smedly's, incoming basket. Through the plate glass window he sees the yellow-wheeled cart near his Arcade level condo. At the rail, the bag lady is looking down onto the street. Something in her hand glints.

Claire, 30, not unattractive in a pinched, repressed way, enters. When he mentions the bag lady and the yellow-wheeled shopping cart, she isn't paying close attention, pre-occupied with a bridal magazine hidden between manila folders.

He watches a Montgomery Security Service man installing a burglar alarm below the railing on the Arcade level. Passing mall workers pay him no attention.

150

Paperwork commands Brandon's morning, but finally he checks his watch and hurries across the arcade level to a popular luncheonette where he takes a seat marked "Reserved." In a leather appointment book, he checks off—11:43-1:10, lunch-Charo's. The waiter, unbidden, brings him lunch.

As soon as Claire is alone in the office, she dials the phone. "No, of course not, Mother. He'll be at Charo's, until 1:10, then take the ferry to Sausalito. I start my vacation Monday so I borrowed Dad's ketch. Friday night, I'll casually wander past at 9:07 just as he finishes dinner at Dumas's. He loves to dive, so when he comments on my naval togs I'll tell him about the boat. He'll want to see it and while I'm showing him around below deck I'll manage to fall into his arms. Nature will take its course, and when the week's up I'll be engaged, and in a month I'll be Mrs. Brandon Harriman.

* * * * * *

That same afternoon, in a meticulously clean and shadowless storage unit, Brandon polishes a full-sized candy-apple-red Jag XK fiberglass car body. It's the real thing scaled up from the model in his condo. The body shines in its multi coats of metallic lacquer. The frame and interior await marriage to the body, but there is no visible means of propulsion

151

CHAPTER-2
DEJA VU ALL OVER AGAIN

At 6:27 the next morning, Brandon sees the same stooped, filthy, ragged, bag lady, and the yellow-wheeled cart near his Arcade level condo. Through the telescope, he recognizes binoculars in her hand. He follows her line of sight to an armored car delivering a package to Jay's Jewelry and Jems. A block behind, a dark blue Plymouth flashes a narrow beam laser signal. Somehow she returns it. The guard leaves the jewelry store, climbs into the armored car, locks its double doors and guides it into light traffic.

Rushing down the stairs, Brandon opens his door just as the woman passes. He grabs her arm and easily pulls her inside.

"Let me go, you creep, or I'll call the police."

"Go ahead." Furtively, she looks around the condo, but makes no move toward the phone easily within reach. The photo of an attractive young woman in flight uniform beside it gets no more than a glance. "Some men were following me. I was scared. Many street people have been mugged lately."

"Yes, I think I saw the culprits. They were in a blue Plymouth."

She seems unsure of her next move, but gains confidence from his non-belligerent posture.
"Ye...No! This was a yellow Ford." She starts crabbing her way toward the door. "Well, have a nice life. I'm gone."

With his hand lightly on her arm, he blocks her path. "I don't think so."

She jerks, trying to escape. The ratty coat she's wrapped in tears away. It no longer hides a lush body.

The filthy hands and face extend only into the covering of ragged clothing. "Kidnapping's a federal offense, you know?" Standing straight she's not much taller than when stooped over. In impotent fury, she stamps her foot. The movement causes the stringy wig to slip, disclosing a grime-streaked young face. "It's no crime to be poor."

He pulls off the gray wig. Released from capture, lustrous, dark hair falls to her shoulders. "That's lame, because I'm onto your plan."

"I don't know what you mean."

Not even bothering to answer, he just smiles. Through the window, he sees the blue Plymouth flash its laser light. It doesn't get the expected response.

Quickly trying to adapt to this unexpected complication, she glances at his desk calendar. "My God, you have to write all that stuff down? Monday through Friday you have breakfast at Starbrite, lunch at Charo's. Saturday and Sunday it's brunch at..."

He opens her plastic garbage bag and finds bottles, aluminum cans and newspapers. Her binoculars are Bausch and Lomb; her watch is a Rolex chronograph. Above the wrist, her arms are clean.

Helplessly, and becoming more nervous, she watches him search. Rapidly, she's growing as frantic as a caged tiger. "You have no life. You live here in building 3, work over there in building 2, probably spend your life within a nine iron shot of both places."

He opens a bag within the bag and finds a cellular phone, her small beam laser flashlight and a change of very fashionable clothing, but no I.D.

"You don't want to get mixed up with me. Your life is well structured. I'm just a complication."

"I said I know what you're up to. Why don't you take a shower, wipe off all that stage makeup and change into your non-bag lady outfit. We'll have breakfast while you try to convince me not to turn you over to the police."

She glows red with fury and with clenched fists, seems ready to attack. Spinning on a heel, she enters the bathroom and noisily locks the door. He selects a new CD and from speakers in every room, there's no escaping Khachaturian's

"MASQUERADE."

On the street below, banners and regalia announce the San Francisco Symphony's Black and White Ball, June 1st. Workers scurry about, making well-choreographed preparations.

In a short red pleated skirt, black hose and patent leather heels, white blouse and black leather bolero jacket, The bag lady of only moments ago is now a model for the good life. Brandon opens a window and from next door, Duke Ellington plays

"SOPHISTICATED LADY."

"If that's your blend-in-with-the-crowd get-away-outfit, I think you should restudy the text book from Burglary 101."

Her dark eyes flash a look of undisguised contempt. Turning his telescope, she pans the street. The blue Plymouth is gone.

He hand-letters a note, pins it to a kitchen bulletin board and helps her down to street-level and a waiting stretch limo. Other than another look of cold hatred, he gets no response from her.

The interior door handle is too far to reach. Seeing no way she'd ever get it open and make her escape, she takes a decanter from the limo's liquor cabinet and fills a glass with Scotch.

"A little early in the day, or is that your norm?"

"What was that note you left?"

"My sister's a flight attendant. She sometimes drops in. I said I'd be out. Now, what's your name?"

He gets no answer, not even a surly glance from her. "Okay, mine's Brandon Harriman."

"Like I care? What kind of a wimp name is that?"

"It was my maternal great-grandfather's surname. He sailed on the *Gjoa* across the Northwest Passage. My grandfather ran a forge and did all the iron work for the cable-car turntables. My father ran a ship chandlery."

"Guess that disproves the American myth that each generation improves."

She takes a long drink and stares out the window as the limo pulls onto the San Francisco Bay Bridge.

He returns the decanter to the liquor cabinet. "This won't change anything, but I guess you know that."

"Can you just accept the fact that at this particular moment, I'd like to get blotto?"

155

She takes a contemplative moment, and then asks, "Where are we going?"

"Fair enough. I'll answer one of your questions and then you'll answer one of mine. A client's horse is running today and he wants me to verify the results I had predicted."

"What are you? A quack psychic or some damn Gypsy?"

"No. I'm a clinical statistician and risk analyst. I make estimates based on the laws of probability. That's two questions I've answered. Now, what's your name and where are you from?"

"I never agreed to your stupid game." She tries to hold out on the grounds of her legal theory. Finally, "Oh, all right. My name is Tori and I'm from Los Altos."

"Tori, that's a beautiful name. It's short for what, Victoria?"
"I don't have to answer that one. I didn't ask you anything."

That's it. If I gave you more, you wouldn't have to buy the book. *Vaughn*

6